SKULL-A-DAY

SKULL-A-DAY

by Noah Scalin

Foreword by Anna Dhody, curator Mütter Museum

CHOP
SUEY
BOOKS
BOOKS

Richmond, VA

Published by CHOP SUEY BOOKS BOOKS, 2913 West Cary Street, Richmond, Virginia 23221

First Edition

10 9 8 7 6 5 4 3 2 1

ISBN 978-0-9960912-0-6
Library of Congress Control Number: 2014943171

design by Noah Scalin/Another Limited Rebellion

Manufactured in China

For Abby, Tatman, and Citizen Agent

"It is not my intention to be fulsome, but I confess that I covet your skull."

— **Arthur Conan Doyle**, The Hound of the Baskervilles

n 2008, a good friend bought me Noah's *Skulls* book for my birthday. Then another friend bought me the same book, then another… By the end of the year, I had four copies of the book. A coincidence? I think not. It shows me that (a) I have a great group of friends that know me very well, and (b) I may need to cultivate other hobbies.

The human skull is, perhaps, the most universally recognized object. Across borders, beyond language, culture, or religion, the skull is known by all. Of course, depending on the context the image of a skull can have different meanings. Put it

on a bottle with some cross bones and you have a poison warning. Run it up a flag pole and you better watch out for pirates.

While the skull usually symbolizes death, mortality, or the fragility of life, it also has other meanings. In Elizabethan England, wearing a ring with a cranium (skull without the lower jaw) could indicate you were a rake, bawd or prostitute. And today, the Mexican holiday of Dias de los Muertos (Days of the Dead) is a joyous and fun-filled celebration of life, family, and food. With sugar skull and skeleton decorations adorning ofrendas (alters) to welcome back the spirits of the

Mütter's Skull of Brains, 2010, detail
Commissioned by The College of Physicians of Philadelphia's Mütter Museum.
Made with 325 slices of real human brains encased in acrylic.

deceased, the idea is not to dwell on death and grieving, but to celebrate life and living.

Noah uses the skull as the visual conduit of his creative mind. What started out as his daily meditation on death took on a force greater than death itself: art. Art does not die. In fact, the Skull-A-Day project took on greater life as more and more people contributed to it. Skulls images from all around the world continue to pour into the website, another example of the universal appeal of the skull. I was honored to have him come speak at the Mütter Museum's Day of the Dead Festival in 2009 and to have him come back again the next year to transform 325 brain slices into an amazing image of a skull. But I am most honored to be able to call him a friend.

The very nature of the skull as the vessel of humanity struck me at a young age. Even today, after handling thousands of skulls in my career, I do not handle one lightly. Always remember, they are human, they are us, and one day, inevitably, we will be them. I have always seen the beauty in skulls, but Noah showed me the art in them as well.

Anna Dhody, *curator*
Mütter Museum, Philadelphia, PA

Introduction

 n June 2, 2007 I had a vision.

I was walking in a park when a fully formed sentence appeared in my head: "I should make a skull a day for a year."

To give you some context, I had been working as a creative professional for over a decade, running my own design firm for six of those years. It was my "dream job," but I was beginning to feel stuck in a rut, losing any of the joy I had found in making a living being creative. I wasn't inspired by the commissions my clients were giving me and I wasn't making work that I loved anymore. To top it off, my one creative outlet outside of work, a rock band, had fallen apart a month earlier after our first big gig. So, on the day I found myself in the park having a vision, I was looking for exactly what it offered: an opportunity to make something I was passionate about, just for myself.

Two days later, I sat in my office and said to myself, "OK, let's do this." I grabbed a sheet of orange paper from my desk drawer and a giant pair of scissors. I crudely cut out a small skull shape from memory. I rotated my chair, stuck the skull on a flatbed scanner, copied it onto my hard drive,

and started a blog called Skull-A-Day. I typed "I'm making a skull a day for a year," posted the first skull, and hit "send." And so it began.

Except that I didn't tell anyone.

Instead, on the second day I decided to push myself even further. Not only would I make a new skull every day for a year, but I would vary the skull image by using different materials and techniques each day. I didn't think this through, which is a good thing, because if I had, I doubt I would've continued with the daunting task that lay ahead.

On the third day, convinced that I really was going to stick with this project, I sent an email to one hundred of my friends explaining what I was up to. I asked if they would help me stay motivated by checking in on a regular basis and sharing the project with their friends. Despite their bafflement, my friends were good sports and did exactly what I asked. One thing led to another, and as the Skull-A-Day blog was shared and reshared, I soon had thousands of people from across the world keeping an eye on my site, asking, "Where's your skull for today, Noah?" I had found my motivation.

I'm often asked, "Did you really make a skull every single day?" In other words, did I cheat? No, I did not. The project was truly about the experience of what happens when you make a commitment to practice something every single day. Realistically, if I had given myself the flexibility to just post seven skulls at the end of each week, I would have waited until Sunday to get started. Instead, I woke up each day, usually having absolutely no idea what I would make, and set out into the world hoping to find inspiration. Those rare mornings when I woke with a notion of the day's skull endeavor, I allowed myself to abandon the plan to explore an unforeseen path.

The reality of a yearlong daily practice meant my existing life had to change. I continued to work a 9 to 5 job doing creative projects for clients, so I began to wake up an hour earlier and tried to make a skull before I started the workday. Some days it didn't work out and I'd spend the whole evening on it. And of course, the entire weekend was fair game. Eventually, the success of the project allowed me to commit more of my time to Skull-A-Day, and I ended up spending an average of two to four hours on each piece.

I travelled a lot that year, both for business and for vacation. When I had no access to my studio or materials, I found I created some of my favorite work. I visited New York City five times during that year and had to constantly come up with new solutions to working in that environment. It didn't take long before I was willing to dig my hands into a public trash can in NYC to find materials. On a Hawaiian vacation, the time differ-

ence forced me out of bed extra early, so I spent the morning hours cutting up avocado or drawing on a coconut. Of course, I made a few sand skulls on the beach, though my wife was adamant that I not spend all day making skulls.

The most difficult day of the project was when I attended a funeral for a good friend who had passed away from brain cancer. At the side of her grave, I reached down, grabbed a handful of the newly churned earth, and brought it home as material to work with. During a "normal" year, I would've never thought to seek comfort in creating a skull. But on this day, in that year, the act of skull-making became cathartic and healing.

Did I ever run out of ideas? Did I ever not want to make a skull? Unexpectedly, I didn't end the year barely dragging myself across the finish line. Instead, I ended with a list of ideas and suggestions I never got to! Yes, of course I was exhausted, as the projects grew in complexity through the year. However, making a skull was always more fun than my regular day-to-day work. Even when I committed myself to a painstakingly monotonous task, like a skull latch hook rug, I still gained perspective from the experience.

Picking a favorite skull proves difficult. Every day, I finished that day's skull excited to start tomorrow's. However, the pieces that stand out to me are the two closest to me, in a very literal way. On day one hundred and one, I commemorated crossing the hundred day mark by giving myself a tattoo of a skull. It's a dramatic reminder of the commitment I'd made and the benefits I'd experienced. I love that I will carry this skull with me until my dying day.

My second favorite piece is the x-ray I took of my own head. Many people suggested the idea, but, clearly, you can't walk into a doctor's office and ask for an unnecessary x-ray. Amazingly, I ran into a family friend at a party who mentioned that she taught medical students how to use x-ray equipment. Yes, she would bring me to the school after hours and let me get an x-ray for the sake of art! I brought a opossum skull to include in the image to show that this x-ray was made specifically for this project, not the product of a doctor's visit. Being able to see my own skull for the first time was a very profound experience.

I remember that year better than any other in my life so far. I was so deeply engaged in being present, looking around my world for opportunities to create, and documenting daily that I ended up with an intense mental journal. Looking back over the images, I can still recall the details of each experience and the people that helped me with great clarity. And I can recognize the exact days when I discovered a new skill or technique that I now use on a daily basis in my personal and professional work.

I gained a lot of amazing and unexpected opportunities from Skull-A-Day including multiple book deals, a visit to the Martha Stewart show, an award from the Young Adult Library Services Association, and art exhibitions in museums and galleries around the world. I've had the honor to speak about creativity with a wide range of audi-

ences, including librarians and young people in schools across the US, incarcerated teenagers in NYC, and designers from the CIA.

One of the coolest things about the project, however, is that it wasn't just about me and my transformative experiences. By sharing my daily practice with the world, I quickly discovered that I made an impact on an entire community of people that had showed up to support my progress. This community was so enthusiastic that they not only commented on the daily work, but began to send me their own skulls as well! I shared one of these on the blog and it opened the floodgates.

I dutifully posted the first few submissions on a Sunday and then every week more and more skulls rolled into my inbox. It was then that I realized what this project really had become: an infinite inspiration loop! I was sharing art that inspired people to make their own art and share it with me, which I then posted, which in turn inspired more people to make and share their art, ad infinitum.

This audience provided me with ideas, encouragement, and materials to work with. I received everything from floppy discs from Australia to soda pull-tabs from Marines in Iraq. My audience participated in contests that I devised, including recording original songs about the project and videotaping themselves performing a dance I diagrammed. In turn, they got me a trophy: the people's choice Webby Award for best Personal Web Site in 2008!

And when my own project drew to a close at the end of the year, 365 skulls later, I didn't have the heart to shut down the site and let this amazing community go. So the very next day, after I posted my 365th skull, I handed the reins over to the public and renamed the site Skull-A-Day 2.0. I assumed that the submissions would eventually just peter out. But they didn't.

This year the site became Skull-A-Day 8.0.

Over the past several years, with the help of three volunteer über-fan editors – Citizen Agent, Justin "Tatman" Lovorn, and Abby Davis – the site continues to grow and reach new people on a variety of platforms. Today, I divide my own time between client commissions, making fine art for exhibitions, writing books, and giving lectures and workshops on generating more creative energy for businesses around the world. I now approach each day with a renewed love for my work, and it all started with a silly little idea when I was at my lowest ebb.

It all started with a tiny orange paper skull.

Noah Scalin
June 2014
Richmond, VA

Skull-A-Day

June 4, 2007

1. Orange Paper Skull

Hand cut with large scissors.
Actual size.

It took me about twenty minutes total to make this piece, scan it, and create the SkullADay.com website on which I posted it. The average time for making and posting pieces during the course of the year was actually two to four hours, with the longest being around ten hours.

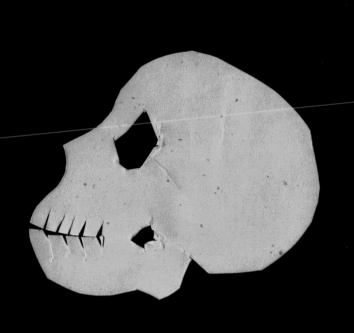

June 5, 2007

2. Blue Rubber Stamped Skull

Rubber stamp ink on paper.
8.5 x 11 in.

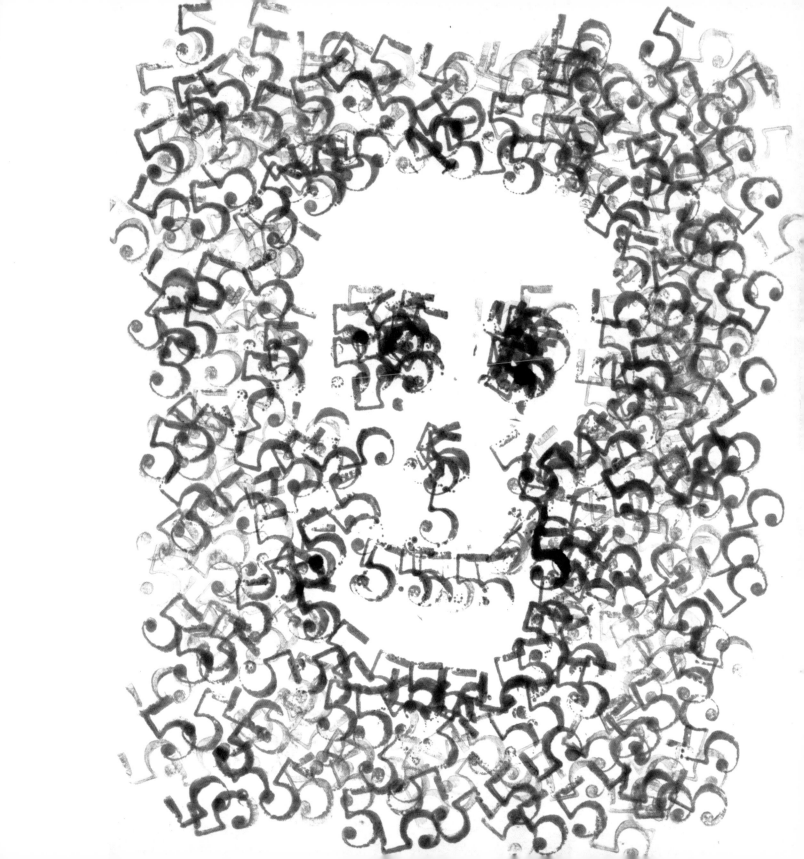

June 6, 2007

3. Sir-Skull-A-Day

Cassette tape cut with scroll saw.

I thought I could make a skull out of a cassette tape and this was the first one I found when I went searching in my basement.

June 7, 2007

4. Silver Wire Skull

Hand-bent picture hanging wire.
1.5 x 1.5 in.

June 8, 2007

5. Crushagami Skull

Folded notebook paper.
1.5 x 1.5 in.

June 9, 2007

6. Turnip Skull

Carved turnip.

SIR MIX-A-LOT
BABY GOT BACK (Album Version)   4:21
CAKE BOY   4:04
YOU CAN'T SLIP   4:58

1
SR

PROGRAMMED, ARRANGED, MIXED, PRODUCED
AND ENGINEERED BY SIR MIX-A-LOT
*Additional Production and Remix by Ricky Crespo
for Cole/Clivilles Music Enterprises
Executive Producer: Rick Rubin

233

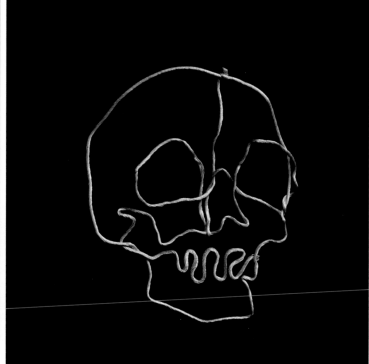

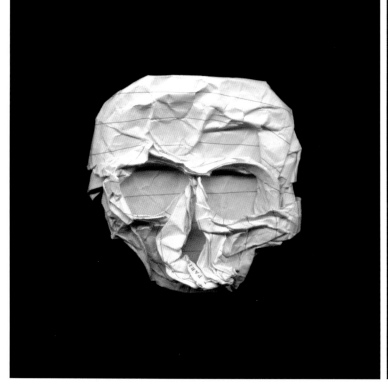

June 10, 2007

7. *Fun With Brad and George Skulls*

Dry brush acrylic on magazine cover.

June 11, 2007

8. *Cardboard Box Skull*

Cut cardboard box.

June 12, 2007

9. *Stencil Skull*

Spray paint on corrugated metal.

This was the first time in the project that I realized I could give away more than just the images of what I was making. I offered up a free PDF download of the outlines for this stencil and just asked that people to send me a photo of how they used it in exchange. I had such a positive response that I intentionally made several other stencils over the course of the project, all of which are still available today. My favorite use of this one was sent from Iraq in 2008 with the following note: "We are a small team of Marines and one civilian who have been operating under the Skulz name for the past five years. We thought it was appropriate to use one of your templates on our HMMWV. We wouldn't dream of destroying or altering US Government property, so we used foot powder…"

Ent ainment
E KL

UN WITH
BRAD&
GEORGE

ITEM# 1223
QTY. 12 PCS
MADE IN CHINA

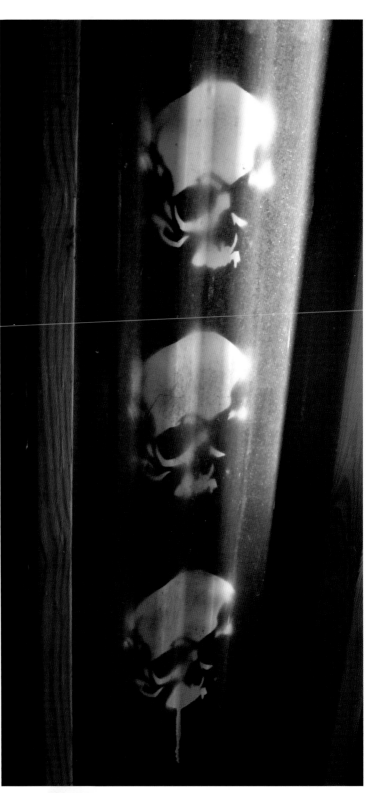

June 13, 2007
10. United Skull of America (above)

Digital Illustration using the 48 contiguous US states.

United Skull of America II, 2009 (right)

Added Alaska & Hawaii two years later.

I was working on a client project, recoloring a map of the United States, when I realized the map was just a puzzle and I could rearrange the pieces. I was pretty excited to share this piece until I remembered that I had only been working with a map of the contiguous US states and I had left Alaska and Hawaii out. It was too late to remake the whole thing and I sheepishly posted the finished piece only to discover that people loved it. In fact, it was so popular that I worried it might be the best thing I'd make all year. I've created several large-scale installations of this piece, including a nine foot tall, laser-cut wooden one for an exhibition at the International Museum of Surgical Science in Chicago.

June 14, 2007

11. Found Metal Skull

Found metal.
8.5 x 11 in.

June 15, 2007

12. Skull Cloud

Digitally retouched photo.

June 16, 2007

13. Plastic Skull Type 1 a.k.a. PETE

Cut from cup lid made of type 1 plastic
(PET/PETE Polyethylene Terephthalate).

June 17, 2007

14. Cutest Skull...Ever!

Digital Illustration.

June 18, 2007

15. Found Skull: "Free"

(left) Remnants of a sticker on a newspaper box at a rest stop on
95 North just south of Washington D.C. and (right) digital illustration.

June 19, 2007

16. 8 X 8 Skull

(left) Digital illustration, 8 pixel by 8 pixel grid.
(right) Arranged Post-It Notes.

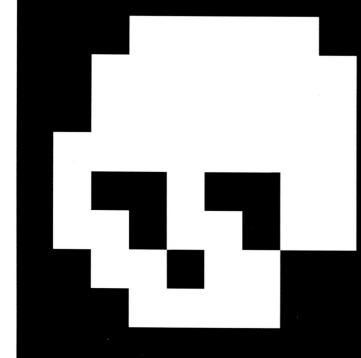

June 20, 2007

17. Pile O'Books Skull

Books cut with a scroll saw.

June 21, 2007

18. Push Pin Skull

Push pins hammered into electrical pole, Richmond, VA.

June 22, 2007

19. Crazy Little Tinfoil Skull...on Toast!

(left) Cut aluminum foil.
(right) Toasted bread made using tinfoil template.

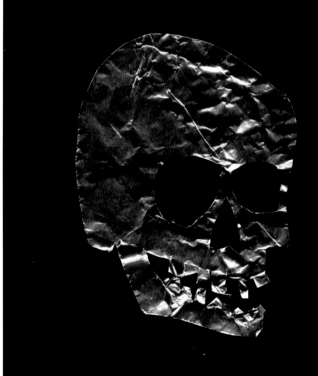

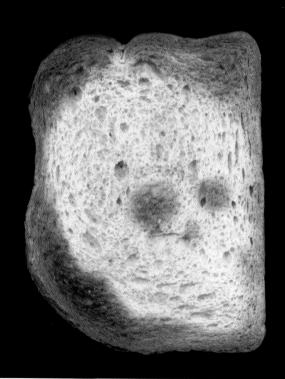

June 23, 2007

20. Eat Your Vegetables Skull

Arranged vegetables.

Inspired by the work of Giuseppe Arcimboldo.

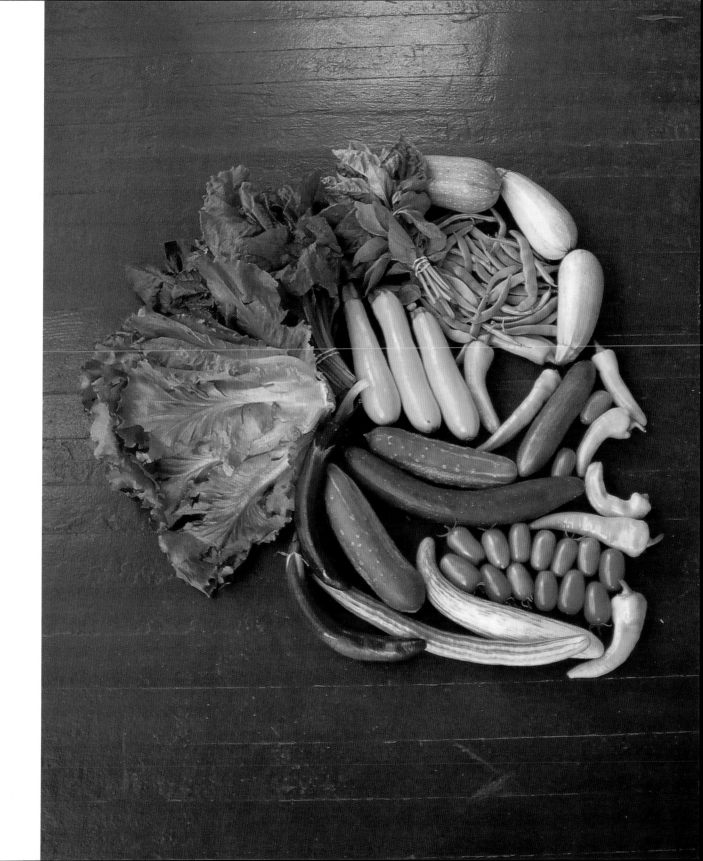

June 24, 2007

21. What's For Breakfast? Skull Pancakes!

Pancake batter, cooked.

June 25, 2007

22. Small Wooden Skull

Carved found wood.

June 26, 2007

23. Mr.(Foam) Peanut (Skull)

Foam packing peanuts and hot glue.

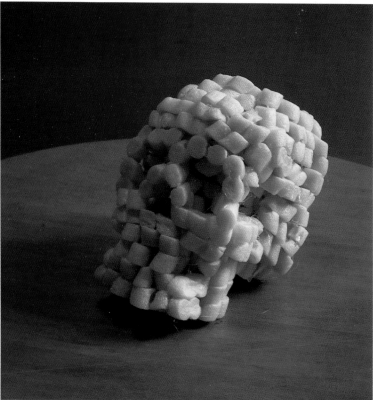

June 27, 2007

24. *(A Sense of) Closure Skull*

Three bread bag closures and one twist tie.

June 28, 2007

25. *Introducing The Skoon (Skull + Spoon)*

Plastic spoon cut with X-Acto knife.

June 29, 2007

26. *Sugar Skull*

Sugar shaped with knife.

(below) In situ at Kramerbooks & Afterwords Cafe,
Washington, D.C.

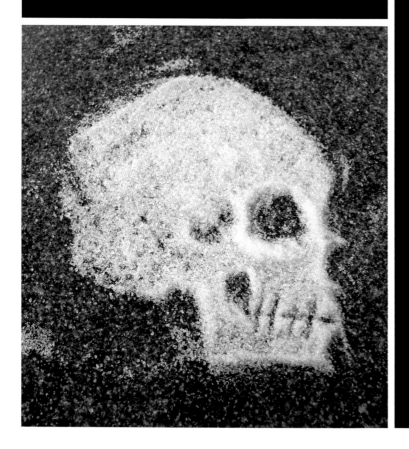

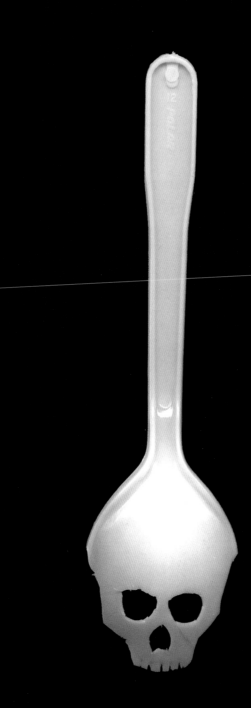

June 30, 2007

27. Shredded Secret(s) Skull

Woven shredded receipts and checks.

July 1, 2007

28. Found Metal Skull #2

Found metal, cut and bent with chisel and pliers.

July 2, 2007

29. Shadow (of a Doubt) Skull

Diffused sunlight on wall.

July 3, 2007

30. 45 Minutes of Cartoon Skulls

Ink on paper. Continuously drawing for 45 minutes.

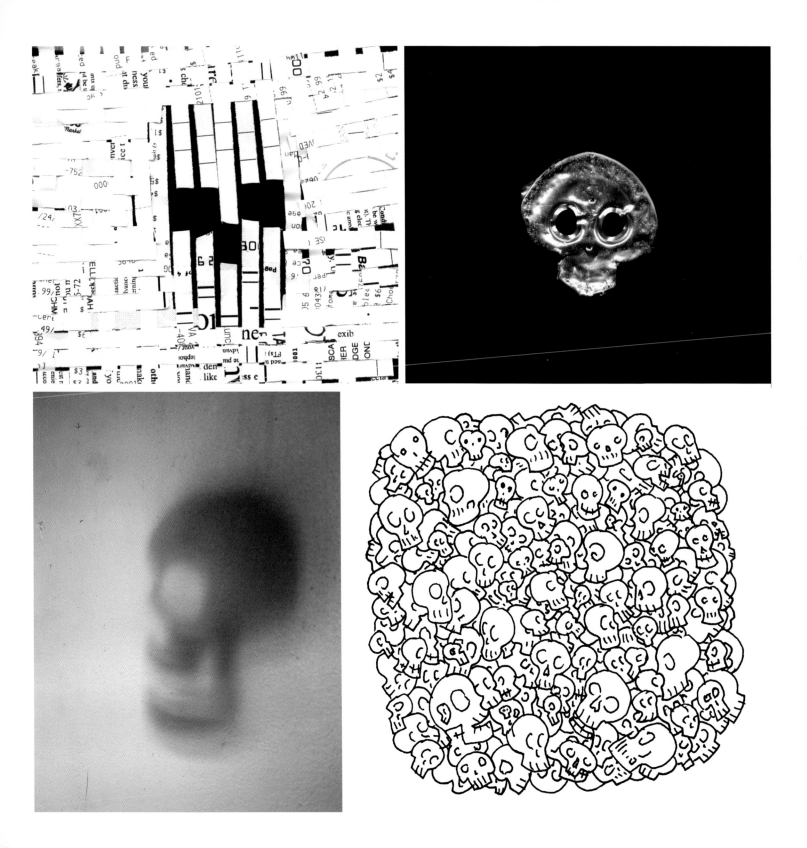

July 4, 2007

31. Plastic Bag Skull

Plastic bag and tape.

July 5, 2007

32. Interlocking Skull

Skull designed for tessellated interlocking pattern,
filled with selfsame pattern.

Inspired by the work of M.C. Escher. Shortly
after I started posting my skulls, a mysterious
regular commenter showed up who signed all
of his notes with different names that included
the letter C. Eventually, he identified himself as
Citizen Agent with a photo of himself wearing
a mask made from this image. I invited Citizen
Agent to become one of the volunteer editors for
the site when it entered version 3.0.

July 6, 2007

33. Libro del Cráneo (Book Skull #2)

Book cut with scroll saw.

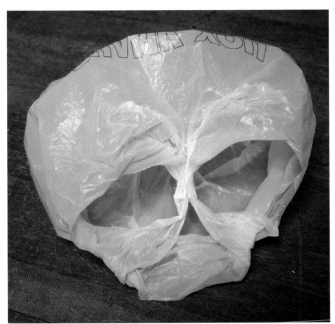
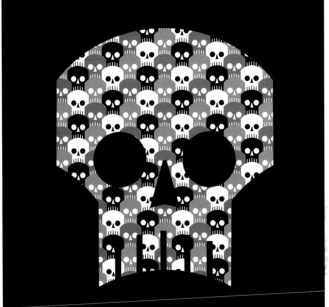

July 7, 2007

34. Baby Toy Skull

Machine sewn fabric.

My friend Chris Boarts-Larson kindly let me use her son Stig as a model this day, so I gave them this piece in thanks.

July 17, 2007

44. "In The New" Crossover Skull

Ink on hand.

Jen MacNeil was also doing a one-year daily project blog in 2007. In her case it was about doing something new every day for the year leading up to her 30th birthday. Since she was based in NYC, we decided to meet up for lunch and do a crossover post.

July 18, 2007

45. Skull Bulb

Holes drilled in light bulb.

This was the only survivor of 8 attempts.

July 19, 2007

46. Soy Sauce Skull

Soy sauce on plate arranged with chopstick.

July 20, 2007

47. Twig(gy) Skull

Arranged found twigs.
Approx. 15 x 15 in.

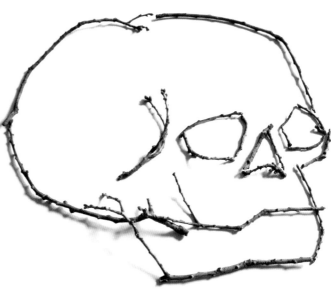

July 21, 2007

48. L33T Skull

Arranged computer keys.

July 22, 2007

49. Rat Skull Print

Linocut print.
4 x 5 in.

July 23, 2007

50. Skull Sponge (a.k.a. Skunge)

Sponge cut with X-Acto knife.
(below) Sponged paint on paper.

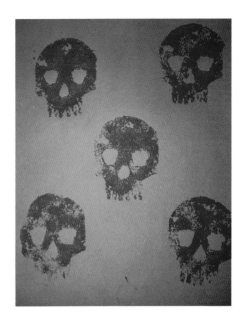

July 24, 2007

51. Watermelon Skull

Carved organic watermelon.

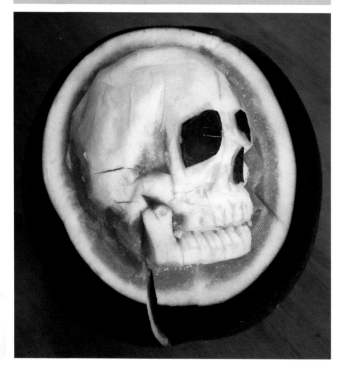

July 25, 2007

52. Splatter Skull

Splattered ink on paper.

July 26, 2007

53. Bar of Skull

Carved bar of soap.

July 27, 2007

54. Wood Burning Skull

Wood burning tool on pine.
Approx. 4 x 4 in.

July 28, 2007

55. Scratchboard Skull

Scratchboard.
Approx. 4 x 6 in.

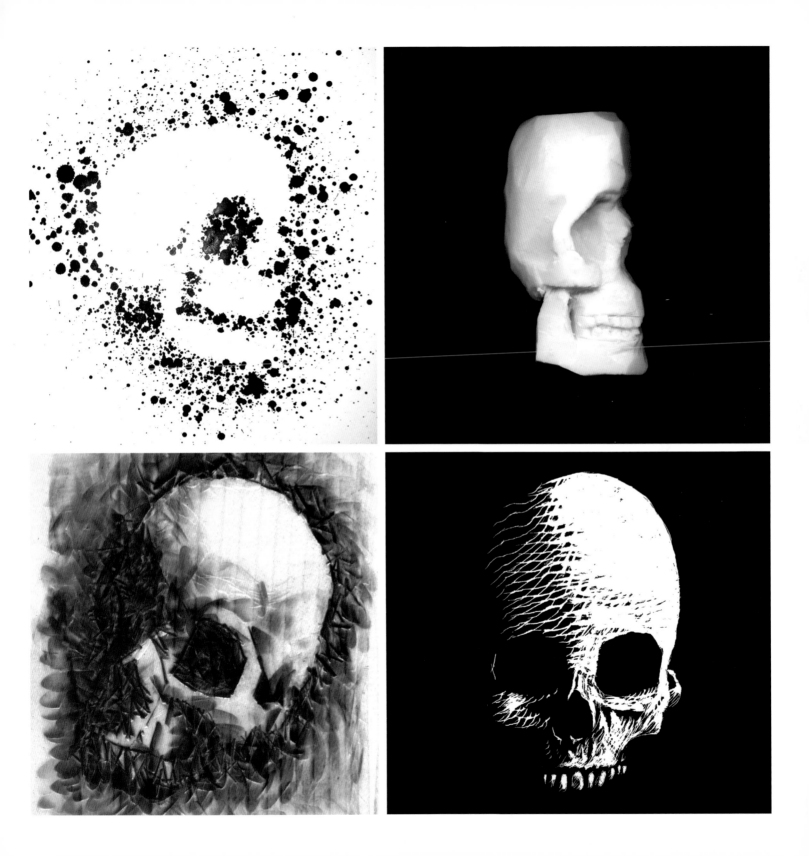

July 29, 2007

56. Face Paint Skull

Face paint on skin.

Modeled by my wife Jessica.

July 30, 2007

57. Plastic Skull Type 6 a.k.a. "Poly Styrene"

Cut cup made of type 6 plastic (polystyrene).

July 31, 2007

58. Duct Tape Skull

Duct tape.
5 x 4 x 5.5 in.

August 1, 2007

59. Sketchy Skull

Charcoal on paper.
7 x 9 in.

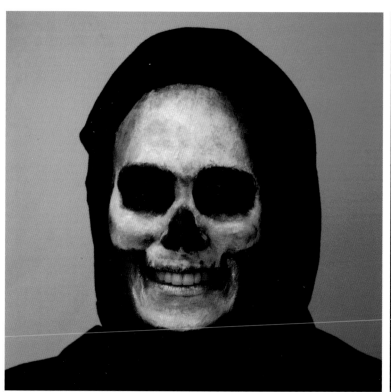

August 2, 2007

60. Flower Skull

Arranged flower petals.

This is the first piece from the project that was licensed for use in another place. One of my former students was working for a design firm that had Poetry Magazine as a client, and he used it on the cover of their December 2007 issue.

August 3, 2007

61. (Hit the) Nail (on the) Skull

Arranged 6d two-inch bright common nails.

August 4, 2007

62. Steel Wire Frame Skull

Bent 20 gauge steel wire.

August 5, 2007

63. Collection Mosaic Skull

Digital photo mosaic of photos of every skull I owned.

August 6, 2007

64. Take Two Skulls...

Carved vitamin supplement pills.

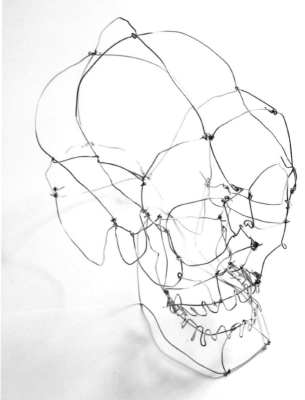

August 7, 2007

65. *Helvetiskull*

Arranged type.
Helvetica Neue, 25 Ultra Light, 35 Thin, 45 Light, and 55 Roman.

August 8, 2007

66. *Sparkler Skull*

Long exposure photography of sparkler.
(below) Alternate shots.

August 9, 2007

67. *Skull Pencil (Skencil or Penskull?)*

Carved pencil (2 views).

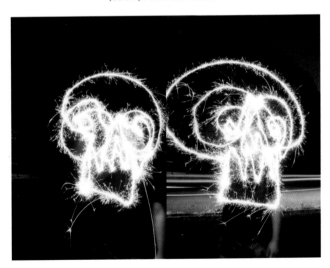

It took about 30 tries to get a handful
of usable results.

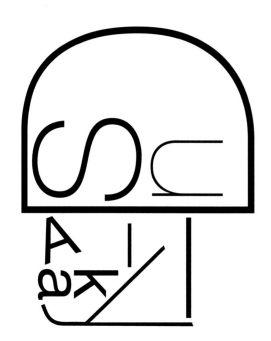

August 10, 2007

68. Rice Skull

Uncooked rice arranged with a chopstick.

August 11, 2007

69. (50) Art-O-Mat (Shrunken) Skulls

Sharpie Marker on shrink film (edition of 50).

I created an edition of these to barter with other artists at the Art-O-Mat 10th Anniversary Celebration/Swap in Winston-Salem, North Carolina. Art-O-Mat is the creation of artist Clark Whittington who recycles cigarette vending machines into art dispensers. The ones that didn't get snapped up that day were given away as contest prizes on the Skull-A-Day site.

August 12, 2007

70. Shoelace Skull

Arranged found shoelace.

August 13, 2007

71. Paint Scratch Skull

Scratched paint on porcelain bathtub.

This piece was made in an old bathtub in my house where we cleaned paint supplies. The eyes were left by two paint rollers that had been stood on end to dry.

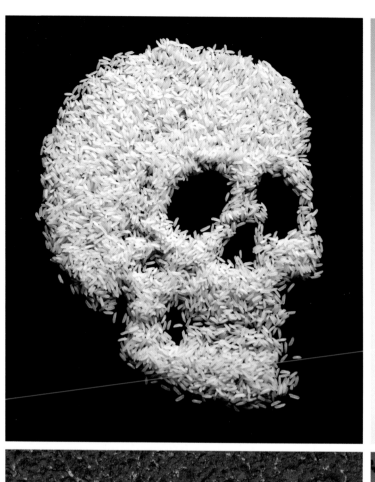
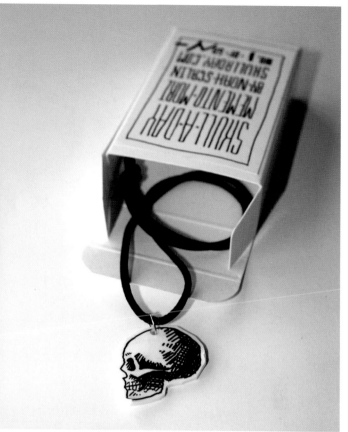
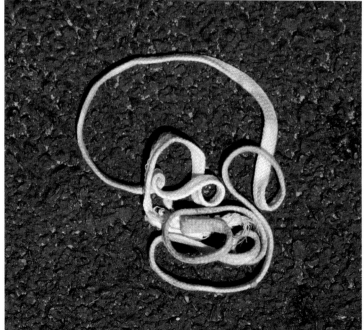

August 14, 2007

72. Papercraft Skull (with Articulated Jaw)

Cut & folded custom paper toy. (below) Pattern diagram.

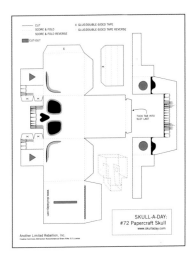

I posted a free download of the pattern for this piece on the site. In return I got images of it used for Christmas tree decorations, as a mobile for a baby's room, as a Halloween costume, as an opera singing puppet, and as a teaching tool in an elementary school art class.

August 15, 2007

73. Watercolor Dog Skull

Watercolor on cold pressed paper.
9 x 12 in.

August 16, 2007

74. Introducing Bubbles the Skull

Arranged soap bubbles in water.

August 17, 2007

75. Expanded T-Skull

T-shirt cut with X-acto knife.

August 18, 2007

76. Mr. Potato Skull Head Stamp Pattern

Potato stamp, paint on paper.

August 19, 2007

77. Skull Sheet

Arranged sheet, hotel room Winston-Salem, NC.

I left this behind to be discovered.

August 20, 2007

78. Sheet Metal Skull

One piece of cut & folded 24 gauge sheet steel.
Approx. 6 x 9 x 4 in.

My ability to complete the Skull-A-Day
project was very much due to collaboration
with friends old and new. In this case, my
friend Philip Perrine let me into his workshop,
gave me access to his tools & materials, and
even helped with the finishing.

August 21, 2007

79. Pasta Skull (Penne)

Arranged uncooked pasta and glitter.

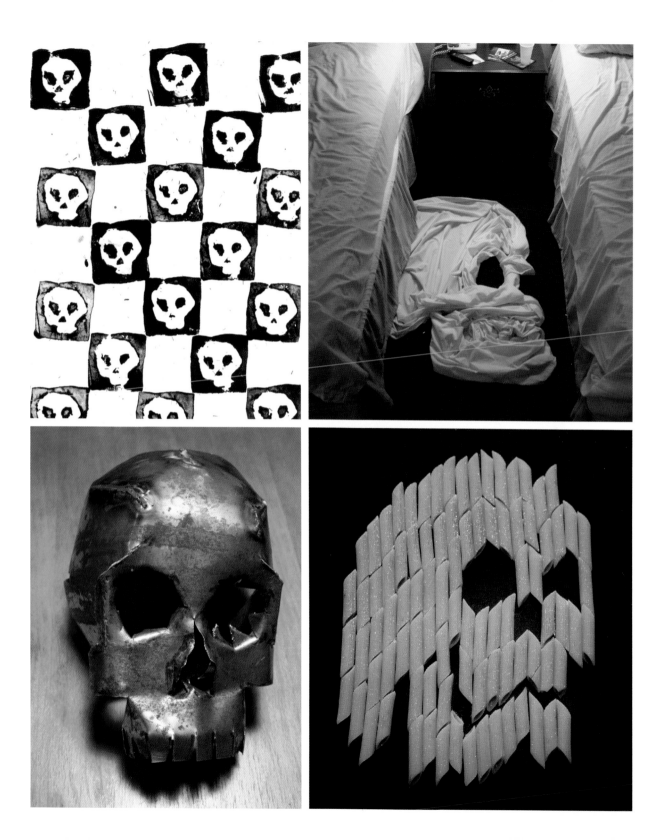

August 22, 2007

80. Peach Pit Skull

Peach pit carved with Dremel tool.

My grandfather used to carve peach pits, so I did this one is his honor.

August 23, 2007

81. Flow Skull

Digital illustration.

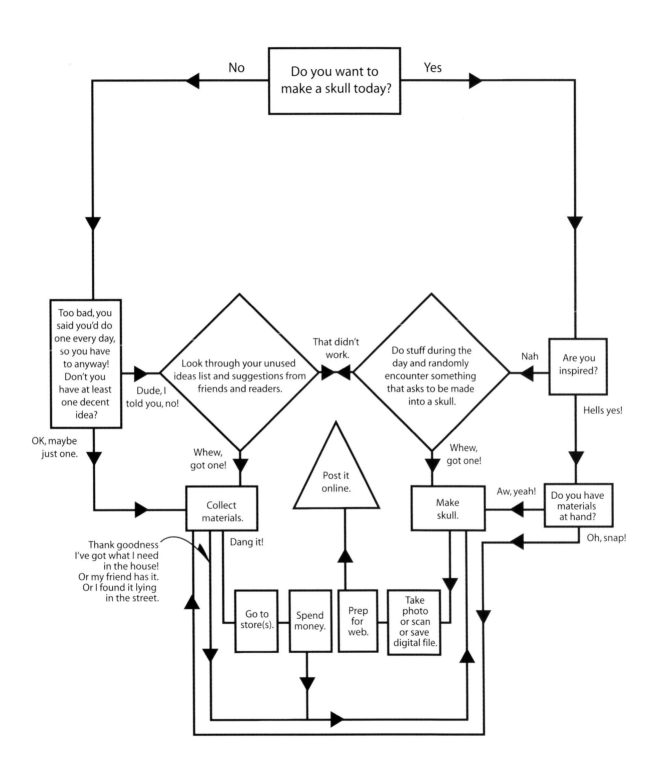

August 24, 2007

82. (She Sells) Seaskull(s by the Seashore)

Seashell cut with Dremel tool.

August 25, 2007

83. Jumbo Bent Wire Skull

Hand bent three gauge wire. (three views)
14 x 9.5 x 5 in.

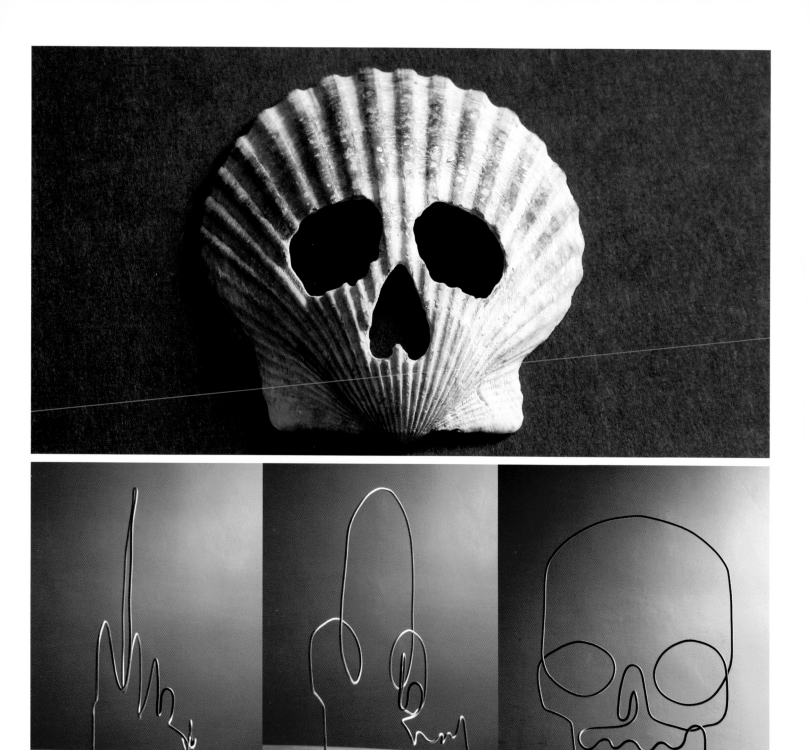

August 26, 2007

84. *Masking Tape Skull*

Hand torn masking tape on cement.

August 27, 2007

85. *Found Bottle Skull*

Arranged and cut found plastic soda bottle,
bottle caps, soda can tab.

August 28, 2007

86. *Drizzled Skull*

Acrylic on cement.
24 x 24 in.

August 29, 2007

87. *Bell Pepper Skull*

Carved bell pepper.

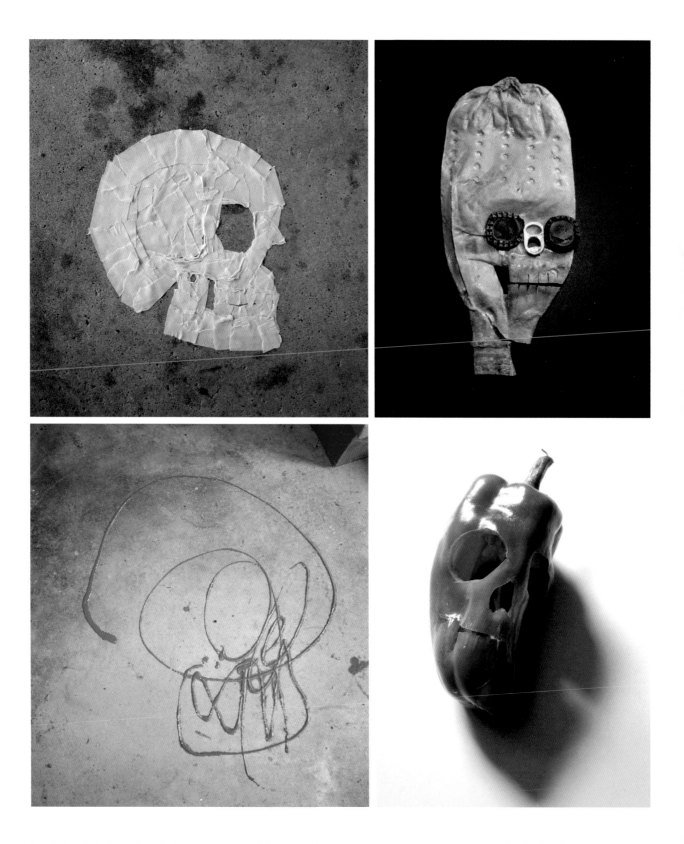

August 30, 2007

88. PB&S (Peanut Butter and Skully)

Peanut butter & fruit spread on bread.

The Martha Stewart Show asked me to
remake this piece when I visited. Martha
actually took a bite out of the finished piece.

August 31, 2007

89. Le Cat Skull

Cut paper.
13 x 7 in.

September 1, 2007

90. Pastel Skull

Soft pastel on pastel paper.

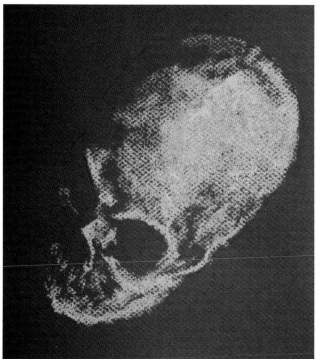

September 2, 2007

91. String of Lights Skull

Arranged string lights on grass.
Approx. 20 x 20 ft.

September 3, 2007

92. Sumi-e Skull

Hand ground ink on rice paper with hand carved chop signature.
9 x 12 in.

This was the best of 45 attempts at a technique I had never tried before. Since I quickly used up all of my existing art skills on such a massive project, many of my days were spent learning new techniques by just doing them.

September 4, 2007

93. "Please, Sir, I Want Some More" Skull

Arranged hot porridge.

September 5, 2007

94. Skullphabet #1

Display capital letterforms based on the Futura Bold typeface.

I offered to make this available as a free font for download if anyone would volunteer to do the programming required. Mark Conahan accepted the challenge, and the font was available on the site less than two weeks later. It's been downloaded hundreds of thousands of times since and I've seen it in use on fliers, logos, and even the tag on a set of skeleton oven mitts.

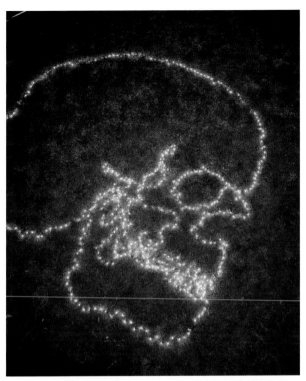

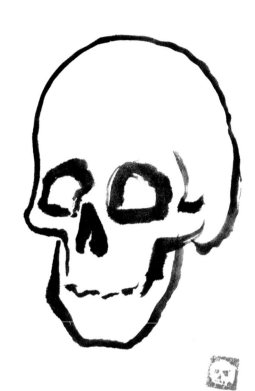

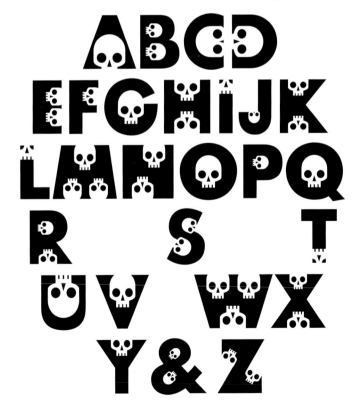

September 6. 2007

95. Leaf Skull

Cut and torn leaf.
Approx. 6 x 8 in.

September 7, 2007

96. Squash(ed) Skull

Carved acorn squash.
(below) As originally posted. (right) Four days later.

September 8, 2007

97. Cereal Skull

Cereal in soy milk.

A fan of the site named Tim created a song for a Skull-A-Day theme contest, and in it he mentioned a skull made out of Cocoa Puffs. Since I hadn't actually made one of those yet, I did this in his honor.

September 9, 2007

98. Take-Out Skull

Carved polystyrene container.

September 10, 2007

99. (Sex, Lies, and) Videoskull

Arranged videotape.

September 11, 2007

100. (I Fell Into a Burning) Skull of Fire

Lighter fluid on concrete.

September 12, 2007

101. Tattoo Skull, Self-Inflicted

Tattoo ink in skin.

After crossing the 100 day mark on the project,
I realized I had to do something momentous.
I had many tattoos before I started Skull-A-
Day, but I'd never given one to myself. Luckily,
I have a good friend who is a tattoo artist, and
she provided the equipment and direction
needed. It took about 15 minutes to do and is
one of the pieces I most often mention when
people ask if I have a favorite from the
entire year.

September 13, 2007

102. Pastel Skull #2

Soft pastel on paper.
Approx 10 x 7 in.

While I was committed to doing a different
skull every day for a year, I had no qualms
with returning to some of the materials and
techniques I used if I wanted to explore
them further.

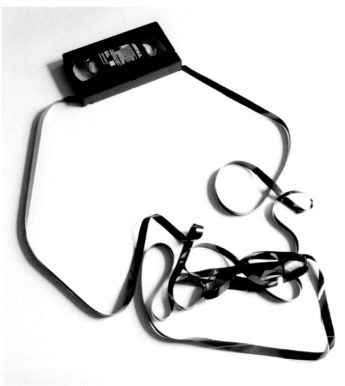

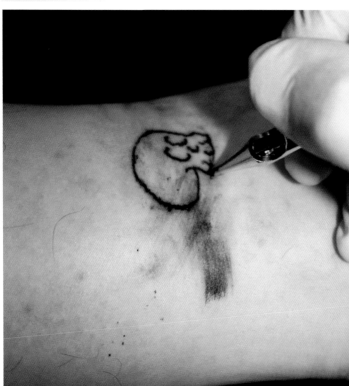

September 14, 2007

103. Paper Napkin Skull

Crumpled paper napkin.

September 15, 2007

104. Vinyl Skull

Vinyl LP cut with scroll saw.

September 16, 2007

105. (I'm a Little) Teaskull

Sculpted pottery clay, unfired.
Approx. 12 x 5.5 x 7 in.

September 17, 2007

106. Found Skull #2: Stormtrooper?

(left) Remnants of a stencil graffiti sticker on a coffee shop window.
(right) Digital illustration.

September 18, 2007

107. Mouse Skull

Computer mouse carved with Dremel tool.

September 19, 2007

108. Shadow Skull #2

Cut paper, tape, cast light on wall.

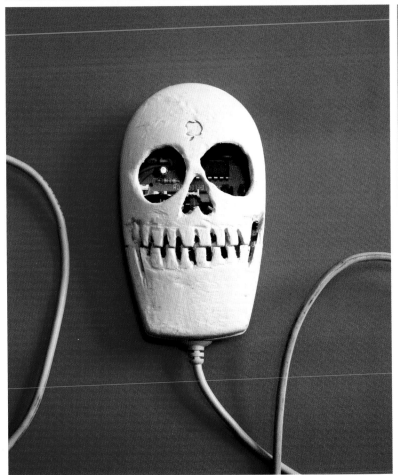

September 20, 2007

109. Jumbo Lace Skull

Arranged lace.
4 x 5 ft.

I was invited to visit the headquarters of the craft website Etsy
in Brooklyn, NY and was given a chance to raid their supply of
materials to create a skull. I ended up tearing into a giant bag of lace
remnants to make this on one of their work tables. They filmed the
process and interviewed me about the project to share on their site.

September 21, 2007

110. NYC Street Trash Skull

Arranged found plastic webbing.
Approx. 2 x 2 ft.

Another visit to New York City and in typical NYC fashion no one cared that I was playing with a piece of trash between parked cars on a busy street.

September 22, 2007

111. New Skull Times

Cut newspaper.

Of all of the public pieces I made in NYC this was one of the few that actually got a rise out of passersby. My sister Mica was my helpful model this day.

September 23, 2007

112. Construction Barrier Skull

Paper taped to construction barrier, 86th St., NYC.

I never did anything that permanently damaged public property, but I definitely worried that I would get in trouble when I did things like this.

September 24, 2007

113. Skull Pick

Guitar pick carved with Dremel tool.

I found this pick on the floor of a bar in NYC.

October 2, 2007

121. Junk Mail Skull = Skunk Mail

Cut junk mail.

October 3, 2007

122. Floppy Skull

Floppy discs cut with scroll saw.

October 4, 2007

123. Blade Skull

Used X-Acto knife blades.

I went through a lot of these in the course of the project, so it was inevitable that they would end up as actual material for a piece. I recently licensed this image for use on the cover of an mystery novel published in Italy.

October 5, 2007

124. Teeny-Tiny Tofu Skull

Carved tofu.
.75 x 1 x .75 in.

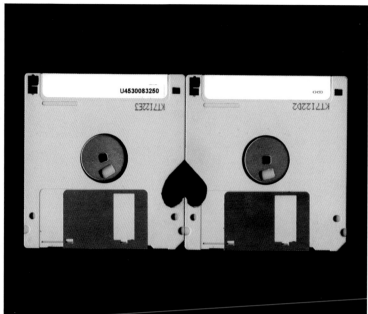

October 6, 2007

125. Broken Glass Skull

Arranged broken glass.
Approx. 3 x 4 in.

October 7, 2007

126. Stained Glass Skull

Stained glass & acrylic.
Approx. 10 x 10 in.

I specifically took a basic stained glass making class to get another skill to use in the project. The teacher said we would have to create a pre-existing pattern, but luckily she allowed me to make something of my own design.

October 8, 2007

127. Skull Lite

Cut found crushed can.

October 9, 2007

128. (No Use Crying Over) Spilt (Soy) Milk Skull

Soy milk.
Approx. 9 x 7 in.

October 10, 2007

129. Skull of Bones

Arranged artificial bones.
Approx. 18 x 18 in.

October 11, 2007

130. (She Just Smiled and Gave Me a) Vegemite Skull

Knife spread Vegemite.
6 x 7.5 in.

I asked my international readers if they liked peanut butter and jelly where they were from and my fans in Australia and New Zealand said they preferred Vegemite. I said I'd never tried it, so Australian fan Beck sent me some to try, along with some other local goodies.

October 12, 2007

131. Acorn Skull (Skacorn? Akull?)

Acorn carved with Dremel tool.
Approx. .5 x 1.25 in.

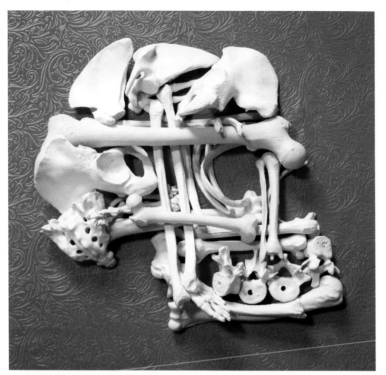

October 13, 2007

132. Candy Skull

Arranged candy.
20 x 26 in.

I created this one to be used on the cover of the Halloween edition of Brick Weekly, a former publication in Richmond, VA.

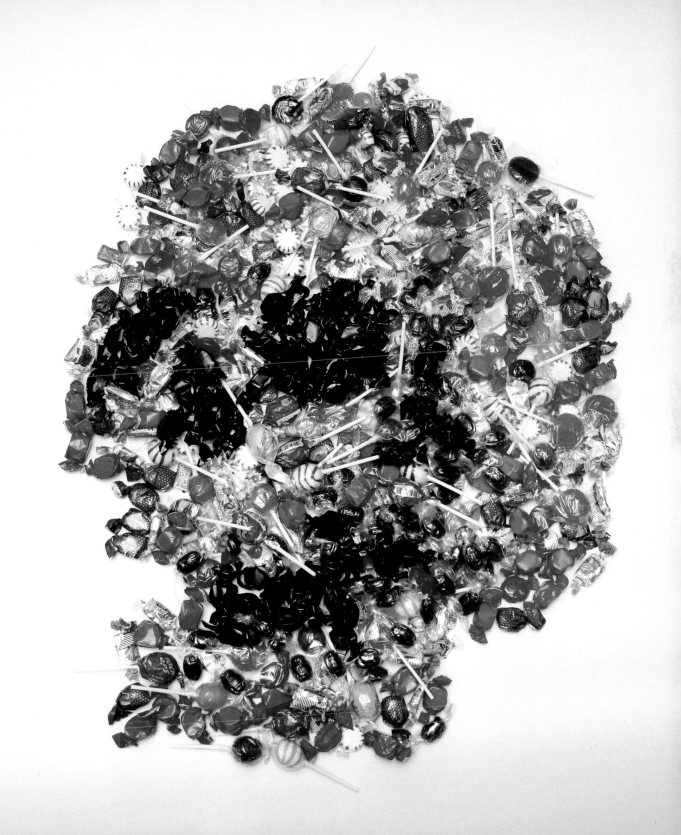

October 14, 2007

133. Bubble Wrap Skull

Bubble wrap and packing tape.
12 x 10 x 12 in.

October 15, 2007

134. Army Men Skull

Arranged plastic army men.
10 x 13 in.

October 16, 2007

135. Leaf Skull #2: Cow

Cut and arranged leaves.
Approx. 4 x 3.5 x 1 in.

October 17, 2007

136. Skullplant

Carved eggplant.

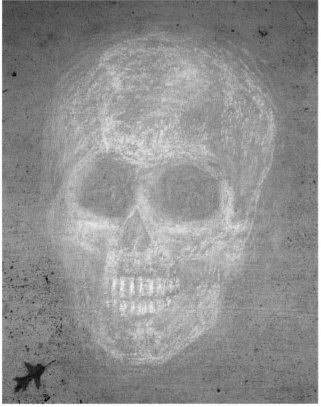

October 26, 2007

145. Balloon Skull a.k.a. "The Dead Balloon"

Acrylic on balloon.

October 27, 2007

146. Baby Belly Skull(y)

Body paint on skin.

My friend Sara Heifetz, pregnant with her first child, asked me to paint a skull on her belly for her costume at a Halloween party at my house that evening. I told her she had to be the skull of that day, to which she replied, "I was hoping you'd say that!"

October 28, 2007

147. Cork Skull

Carved wine cork.

October 29, 2007

148. Paper Doll Skull

(above) Cut paper toy. (right) Digital illustration.

I enjoyed coming up with new ways for people to interact with the work I created during the year. This was another case where I provided a diagram of a papercraft toy for people to download and make themselves.

CUT ——————

FOLD ------------

INSERT TOP OF SKULL

INSERT TOP OF SKULL

INSERT TOP OF SKULL

FOLD BASE
BACK AND
FIT TOGETHER
LIKE THIS

www.skulladay.com

October 30, 2007

149. Cocoa Skull

Stenciled cocoa powder.

October 31, 2007

150. Rice Skull 2: Cooked

Hand-sculpted cooked rice.

I made this at the house of my friends Christi & Russ who dutifully kept it in their freezer for many years after.

November 1, 2007

151. Brown Paper Skull

Torn and folded paper lunch bag.

November 2, 2007

152. Hair Skull

Arranged human hair.

My friends at the Pine Street Barbershop in Richmond, VA were amused but happy to let me take my own hair home after a haircut to make this.

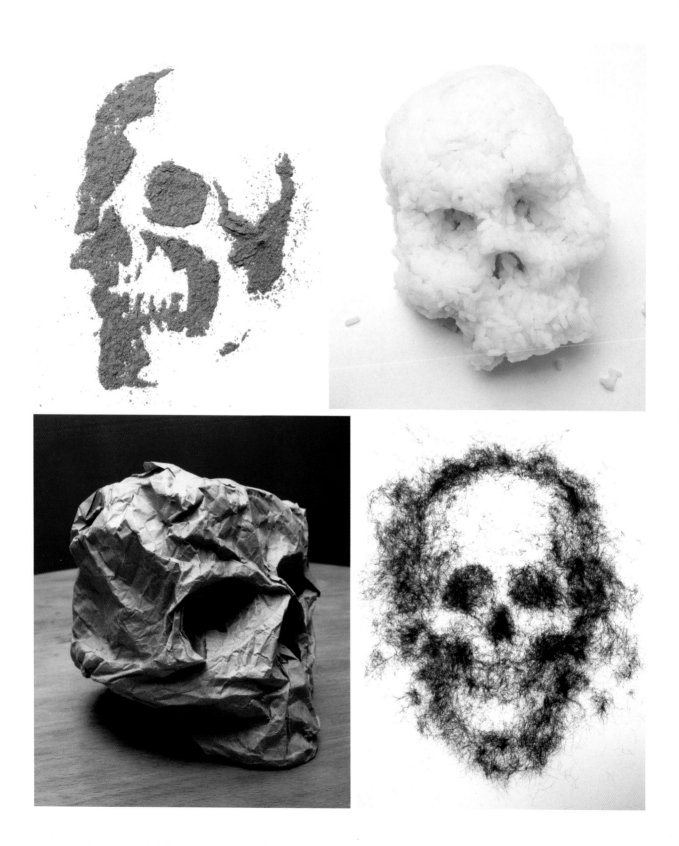

November 3, 2007

153. Sugar Cube Skull

Stacked sugar cubes (and glue).

November 4, 2007

154. Chocolate Chip Skullies

Cookie dough and chocolate chips (baked).

November 5, 2007

155. Wet Paint Skull

Wet acrylic paint on plate.
Approx. 4 x 4 in.

November 6, 2007

156. Onion Skull

Arranged chopped onion.

November 7, 2007

157. Shade(s of Death) Skull

Cut plastic window shade.

November 8, 2007

158. Skullage

Digital collage of Victorian chromolithographs.

November 9, 2007

159. Six-Pack Skull

Torn, stretched, and cut plastic six-pack ring.

November 10, 2007

160. Petroleum Skully

Sculpted petroleum jelly.
5 x 5 x 1 in.

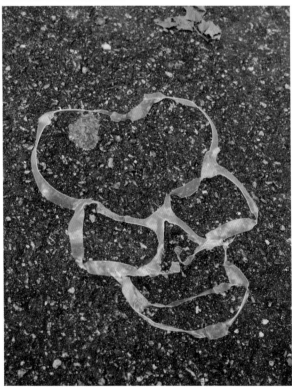
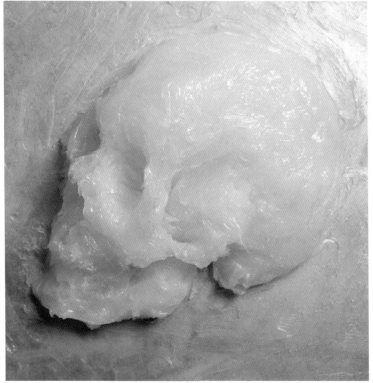

November 11, 2007

161. Latch Hook Skull

Yarn on canvas.
12 in x 12 in.

On one of my many shopping trips for
supplies during this year, I bought a pre-
existing latch hook kit to make a photo-
realistic image of a puppy at a craft store.
I then designed my own pattern based on a
photo I took, using the yarn colors provided.
This was one of the longest projects I did over
the course of the year, clocking in at nine hours
– not including the nap I took to get rid of a
migraine I got from this task.

November 12, 2007

162. (Minty Fresh) Skullpaste

Knife spread toothpaste.

November 13, 2007

163. Skulluminum Foil Ball

Aluminum foil.
5 x 5 x 6 in.

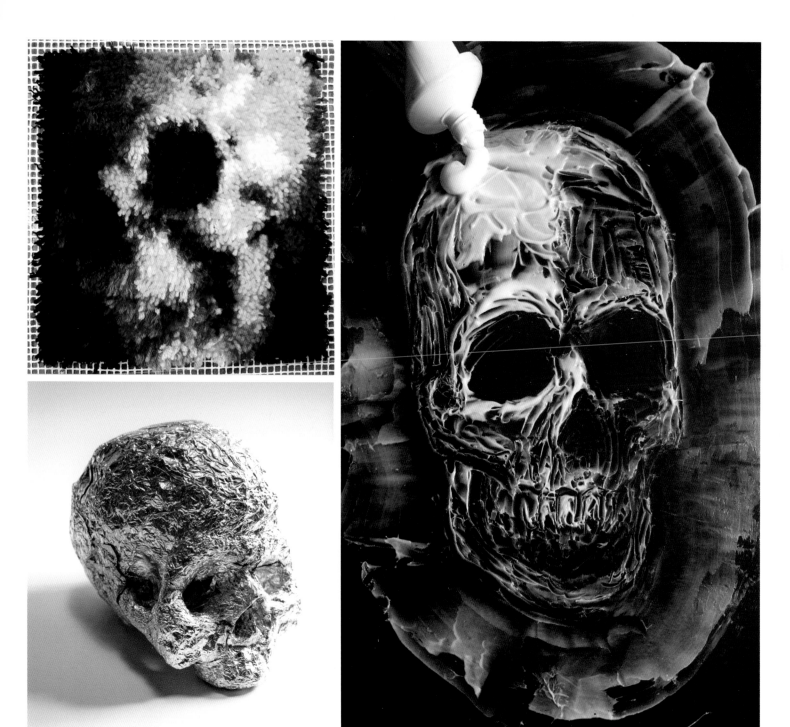

November 14, 2007

164. Action Figure Skull

Sculpted modeling compound. (left) Normal light. (right) Glowing in the dark.
4 in.

November 15, 2007

165. Miniature Skull

Carved modeling compound.
Approx. .5 x .5 x .375 in.

November 16, 2007

166. Fused Bead Skull

Fused plastic (#4 LDPE) beads.
5.5 x 5.5 in.

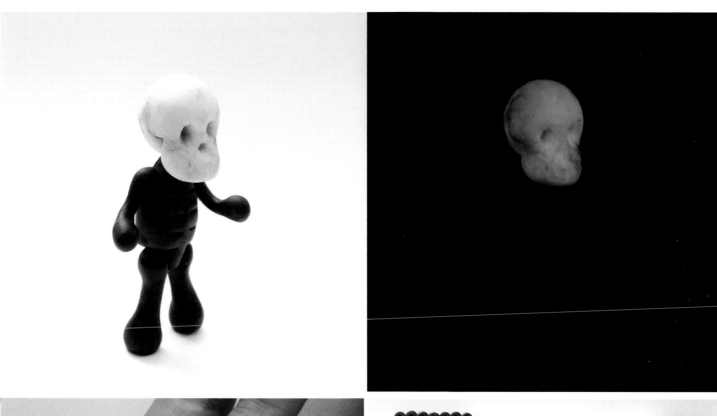

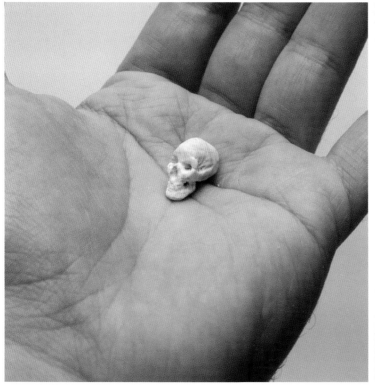

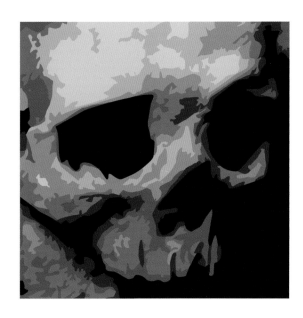

November 17, 2007

167. Skull By Numbers

Digital illustration. (above) Completed.

I thought it would be fun to give people a bit of a surprise if they actually attempted this task. I added what looked like a couple of skulls to the interior of the pattern. When painted those skulls disappear and the one above appears. I didn't reveal the final image online until people had a chance to try it out.

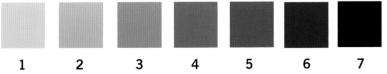

November 18, 2007

168. (Escape to) Skull Mountain

Papier-mâché and mixed-media.
Approx. 11 x 5 x 8 in.

I've always loved making models and at one point dreamt of
becoming a special effects model maker for movies. I used an old
mirror to create the rippled looking water, sandpaper made the
grassy land, and cornstarch served for snow. Several people thought
this was a photograph of a real place.

November 19, 2007

169. Found Skull #4: Apartment Grayskull

(left) Photograph. (right) Digitally colored ink drawing.

My friend Russ Gautier told me about a building not far from
where I lived that he and some other friends called Castle Grayskull.
True enough, there was a distinctive skull face on one side of the
structure which I documented and then used for inspiration for an
illustration.

November 20, 2007

170. Skullghetti & Sauce

Arranged spaghetti and sauce.

November 21, 2007

171. Finger Print Skull

Ink on finger monoprint.

November 23, 2007

173. Sand Skull 1

Hand sculpted sand, Bellows Beach, O'ahu, Hawaii. (below) In situ.
Approx. 3 x 3 ft.

November 22, 2007

172. Paper Napkin Skull 2

Crumpled paper napkin.

Thanksgiving Day was spent traveling to
Hawaii for a one-week vacation. This was
created during a layover between flights at the
Dallas-Fort Worth International Airport.

November 24, 2007

174. (The) Coconut Skull (Doesn't Fall Far From the Tree)

Ink on coconut, Kaneohe Bay, O'ahu, Hawaii.

November 25, 2007

175. Flower Skull 2

Arranged flowers, Kailua, O'ahu, Hawaii.
Approx. 9 x 9 in.

November 26, 2007

176. Toothpick Skull

Arranged toothpicks, Kailua Kona, Hawai'i, Hawaii.

November 27, 2007

177. Lava Stone Skull

Arranged coral on volcanic rock, Pu'uhonua o Honaunau National
Historical Park, Kona, Hawai'i, Hawaii.

November 28, 2007

178. Candy Cane Skull

Arranged candy canes.

November 29, 2007

179. Avocado Skull

Carved avocado.

December 1, 2007

181. Skullar Bill

Folded U.S. one dollar bill.

November 30, 2007

180. Sand Skull 2

Hand sculpted sand, North Shore, O'ahu, Hawaii.
Approx. 2 x 2 x 2 ft.

I made this on a plane somewhere in the air between Phoenix, AZ and Philadelphia, PA on our return trip from Hawaii. I shot it on the tray table using just the reading light. The older gentleman sitting next to me seemed pretty baffled, so I explained that I was making art, which seemed to satisfy him. Later he said, "At first I thought you might be crazy!"

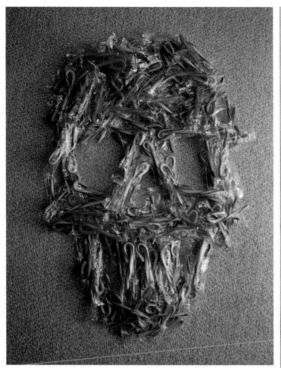

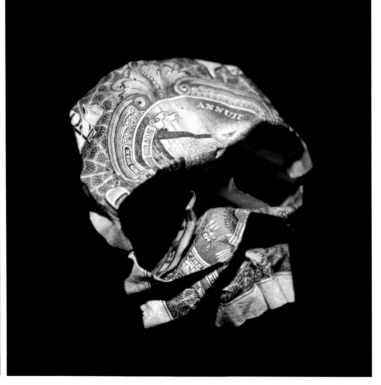

December 3, 2007

183. Bottle Cap Skull

Bottle cap cut with Dremel tool.

December 2, 2007

182. Stipple Skull

Stippled ink on illustration board.
8 x 4.5 in.

December 4, 2007

184. Ink & Tray Skull

Printing ink on etched polystyrene tray.
8.25 x 5.75 in.

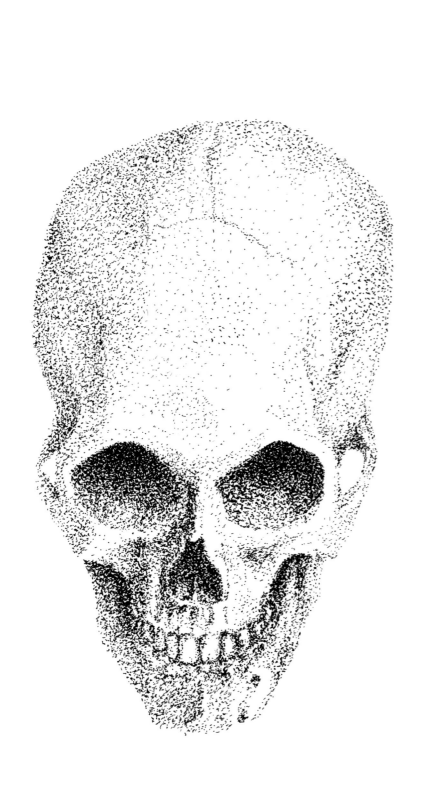

December 5, 2007

185. (House of) Wax Skull

Dripped wax on board.
Approx. 7 x 7 in.

The ability to make gray colored wax with soot by tilting the white candle I was using was a happy discovery during this process.

December 6, 2007

186. Egg Skull

Eggshell drilled with Dremel tool.

December 7, 2007

187. Skull Clips

Bent 20 gauge steel wire.
Approx. 1 x .625 in.

December 8, 2007

188. (Back to) Skull Notebook

Erased paper notebook cover.
Approx. 3.5 x 5.5 in.

A technique remembered from school days.

December 9, 2007

189. Skull-Aid

Arranged adhesive bandages.
Approx. 13 x 11 in.

December 10, 2007

190. Date Skull

Carved Medjool date.
Approx. 1.5 x .75 x 1 in.

December 11, 2007

191. 13 Line Skulls

Digital gesture drawings using computer mouse.

December 12, 2007

192. Ornament(al) Skull

Digital illustration made from arranged
Victorian decorative border elements.

This was one of the most popular creations of
the year. I made my own t-shirts and prints of
it and it was licensed for use on both a book
cover and a sweater. It was also used without
permission on t-shirts that were sold at a
major retailer. Luckily, a fan tipped me off
when he discovered them on sale. It was the
first time I had to engage the use of a lawyer to
protect my intellectual property. Sadly, it was
not the only time this happened.

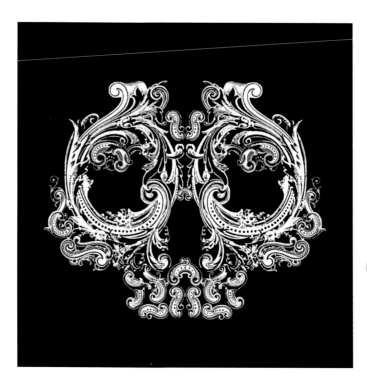

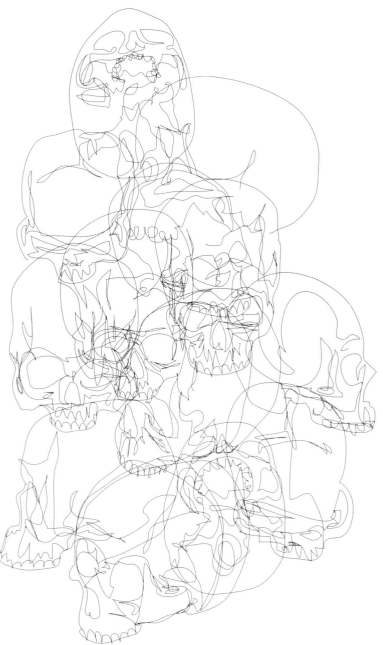

December 13, 2007

193. Felt Skull Patch

Cut & glued felt on jacket.
Approx. 8.5 x 11 in.

For a Current TV segment on Richmond, Virginia, I was visited by J.T. After he interviewed me and modeled this piece, I let him keep the jacket.

December 14, 2007

194. Pastel Possum Skull

Pastel on paper.
Approx. 4 x 7.5 in.

December 15, 2007

195. Silkscreen Skull

Metallic silver and red silkscreen ink on paper.
18 in x 24 in.

The top layer is from a photo I took in the Paris Catacombs. The bottom layer features a new arrangement of the skulls from day 191. My friend Spencer Hansen taught me how to silkscreen and let me use his equipment to make a small edition of this print.

December 16, 2007

196. Glass Mosaic Skull (Unfired)

Arranged glass. (below) Fired.
Approx. 4 x 6 in.

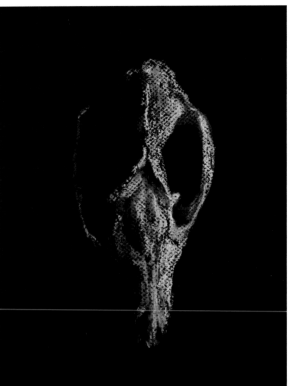

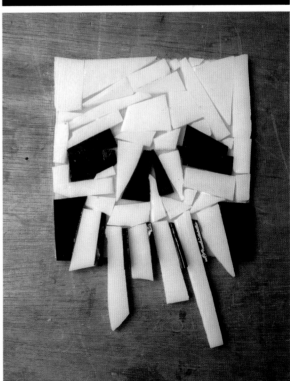

December 17, 2007

197. Tooth Skull a.k.a. Cavity Creep

Human tooth carved with Dremel tool.
Approx. 3/4 x 3/8 x 1/2 in.

This is one of my actual wisdom teeth. I had them pulled when I was in high school and held on to them ever since.

December 18, 2007

198. Emerging (or Sinking) Skull

Sculpted pottery clay, unfired.
Approx. 6 x 4.5 x 1 in.

December 19, 2007

199. Soundproof Skull

Cut and carved acoustical tile.
15.5 x 16.75 in.

December 20, 2007

200. Two Dollar Skull

200 arranged pennies.

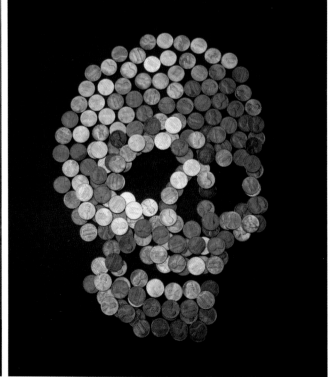

December 21, 2007

201. Tin Can Skull

Hammered, bent, and cut tin can.

December 22, 2007

202. Rub-On Type Skull

12pt Helvetica rub-on type on board.
5 x 5 in.

December 23, 2007

203. Chocolatey Delicious Skull

Arranged chocolate & chow mein noodles.
Approx. 7 x 9 in.

December 24, 2007

204. 24 Karat Skull

Gold leaf on painted wood.
8 x 8 in.

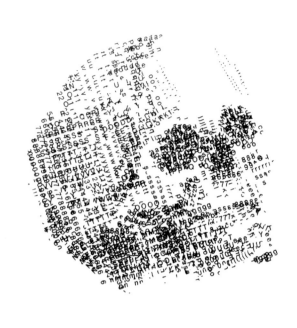

December 25, 2007

205. (Light as a) Feather Skull

Arranged feathers.

December 26, 2007

206. Totally Nuts Skull

Arranged zinc hex nuts.
Approx. 7 x 9 in.

December 27, 2007

207. Stump(ed) Skull

Charcoal on tree stump.
Approx. 3 x 3 ft.

There was a giant tree that had died and was
falling apart in front of my house. During the
project, the city sent a crew out to cut it down.
This piece only lasted a few days before they
came back and ripped out the stump
as well.

December 28, 2007

208. No. 2 Penskull

Arranged number 2 pencils.

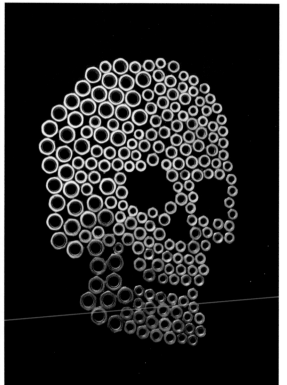

December 29, 2007

209. Caution Skull

Arranged plastic barricade tape.
Approx. 4 x 4 ft.

December 30, 2007

210. Safe Skull

500 arranged condoms.
Approx. 22 x 16 in.

December 31, 2007

211. Etched Skull

Light cast through etched glass.
10 x 10 in.

January 1, 2008

212. Scribble Skull

China marker on paper.
7 x 7.5 in.

January 2, 2008

213. Floppy Skull v2.0

5.25 Inch floppy disc cut with X-Acto knife.
5.25 x 5.25 in.

Skull-A-Day fan Kim from Australia mailed
me this to specifically use in the project.

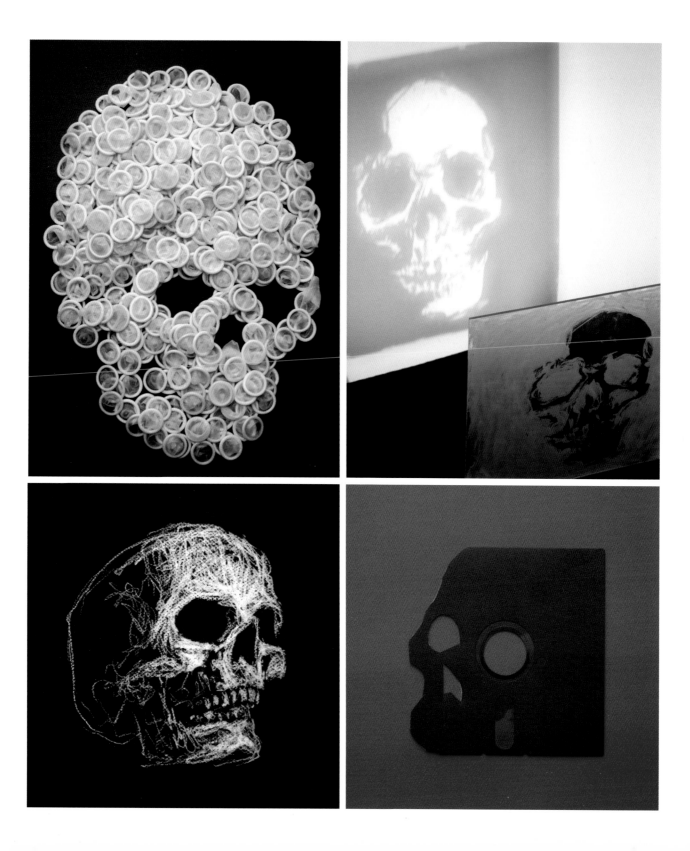

January 3, 2008

214. Numeral Skull

Digital illustration of arranged numbers in Caslon Regular.

January 4, 2008

215. (Break the) Ice Skull

Arranged found ice.
Approx. 8 x 8 in.

January 5, 2008

216. Copper Cube Skull

Hand cut and soldered 18 gauge copper sheet.
1 x 1 x 1 in.

All six sides show a different view of the skull. My friend Carra Rose let me work in her studio, taught me this technique, and helped me do the soldering.

January 6, 2008

217. Cotton Ball Skull

Arranged cotton balls.
14 x 20 in.

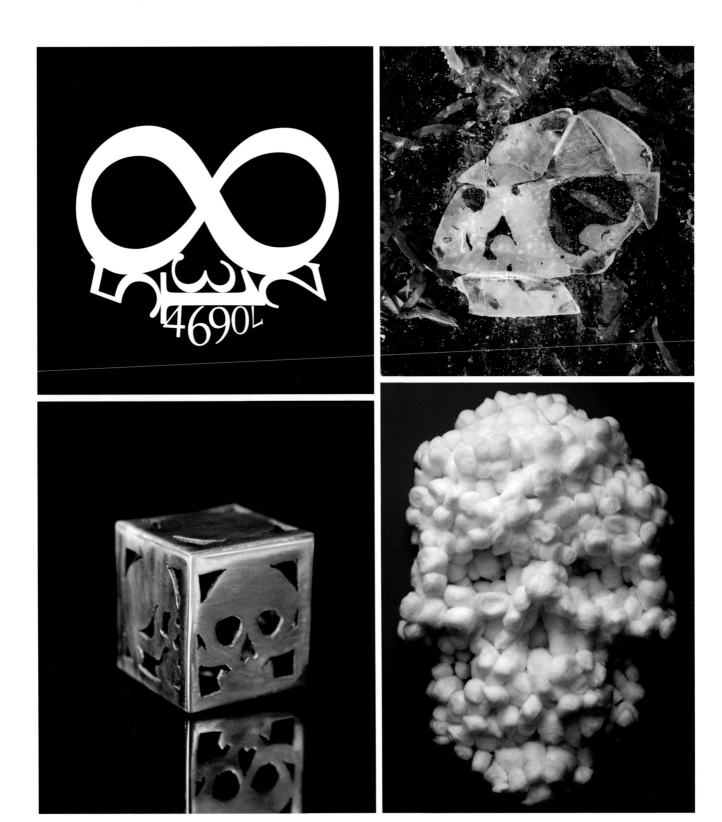

January 7, 2008

218. Found Metal Skull #3

Hammered, cut, & bent found metal.
2 x 2 in.

January 8, 2008

219. Skull-Master

Cut & arranged vintage View-Master slides.

January 9, 2008

220. Five Golden Skulls

One length of hand bent 24 gauge metal wire.
4.5 x 7 in.

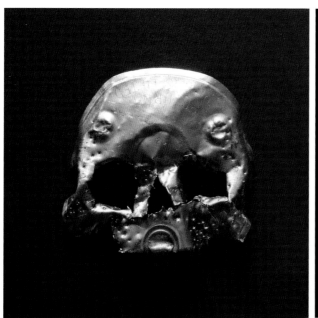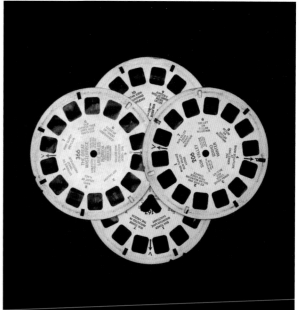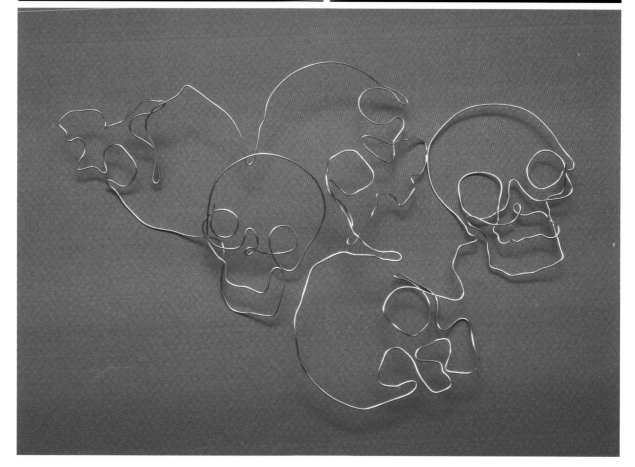

January 10, 2008

221. Lino Skull #2

Linocut print.
8 x 10 in.

January 11, 2008

222. Rorschach Skull

Digital illustration.

Inspired by the famous Rorschach inkblot test.

January 12, 2008

223. Recycled Skull Ring

Cut, soldered, and bent 14K white & yellow gold wedding ring.

My friend Tere Hernandez-Bonét let me into
her jewelry studio and helped me with the
complex process of deconstructing my old
wedding ring into this new creation.

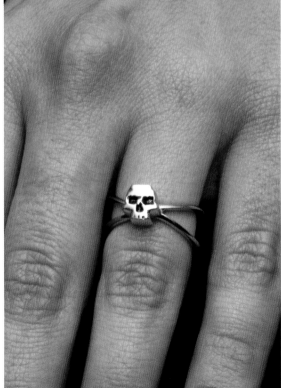

January 14, 2008

225. Headache Skull

1000 arranged aspirin.
10 x 12 in.

January 13, 2008

224. Butternut Skull

Carved butternut squash.
9.5 x 4.5 x 4.5 in.

January 15, 2008

226. Comic Geek Skull

Arranged comic books and toy, Velocity Comics, Richmond, VA.

My friend Patrick Godfrey gave me free reign
in his store to create this piece.

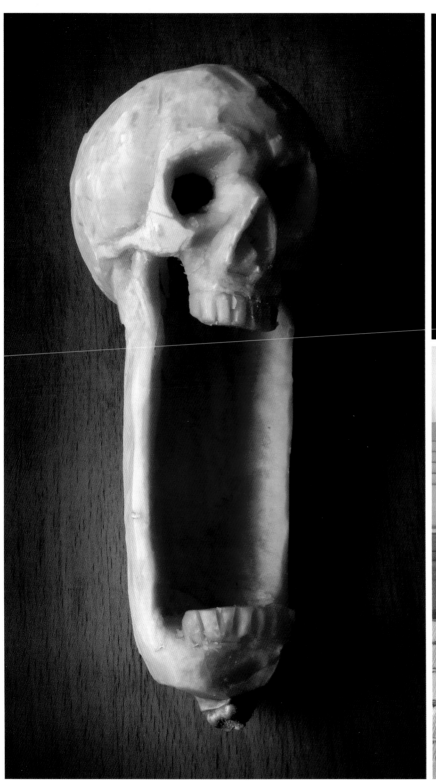

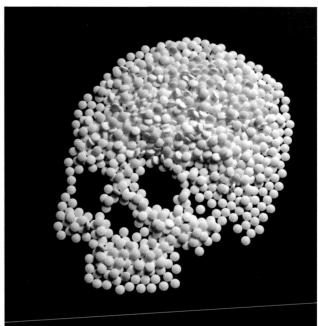

January 16, 2008

227. Stapled Leaf Skull

Torn & stapled leaves.
6.25 x 6.25 in.

January 17, 2008

228. Steam Skull

Steam drawing, Korean restaurant, NYC.

January 18, 2008

229. Lipstick Traces Skull

Lipstick on mirror with model in bathroom, Allure Magazine office, NYC.

My friend Christine Colby invited me to visit me at her job to make
a piece for the project. We decided to sneak into the men's bathroom
with a sample tube of lipstick.

ABC
DEFGH
IJKLMN
OP Q
RS TU
VWX
Y&Z

February 3, 2008

245. Reel-to-Skull

Arranged magnetic tape on reel-to-reel recorder.

February 4, 2008

246. Yarn Painting Skull

Yarn glued to cardboard.
8 x 11 in.

February 5, 2008

247. Valentine's Skull

Acrylic on cut chocolate box.

February 6, 2008

248. Mmmmmm Skull

841 arranged candy coated chocolates.
15.25 x 15.25 in.

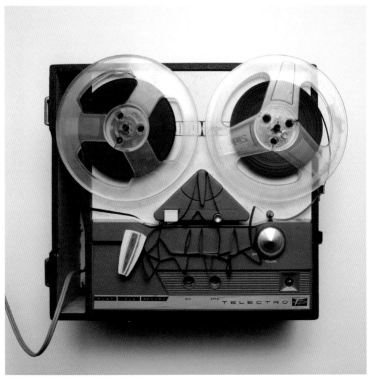
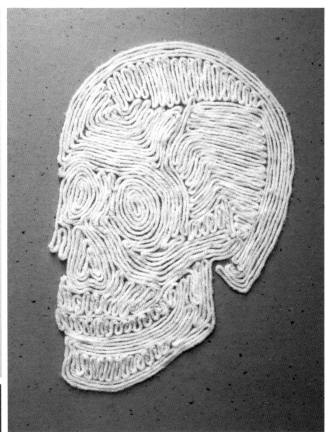

February 7, 2008

249. Flock of Skull

Digital illustration.

More than one person asked how I managed
to capture this photo, assuming that it wasn't a
fictionalized creation.

February 8, 2008

250. Crosskull Puzzle

Functional crossword puzzle.

I was inspired to create this after watching
the documentary film Wordplay and used a
technique described in the movie as a starting
place. I started getting comments from people
who actually managed to solve it within a few
hours of posting it.

February 9, 2008

251. Puzzle(d) Skull a.k.a. Skuzzle

Arranged jigsaw puzzle pieces.
9.5 x 11 in.

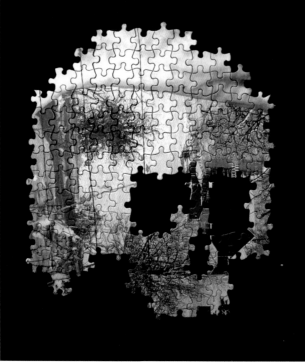

		1	2	3	4	5	6	7	8	9				
	10	11									12	13	
14				15					16			17
18				19						20		
				21								
				22								
			23			24	25					
26	27	28	29	30			31	32	33	34	35
36						37					
	38		39		40	41			42		
43			44		45		46			47	48
49		50	51						52		
	53		54		55		56		57		
	58			59		60		61			
	61										

ACROSS

1 Skull
10 Snobby creative recycler?
14 Command-Z
15 Touched by cat
16 Egyptian cross
18 The knights who say _
19 Untruth
20 Jackson's "Captain _"
21 Jewish state (abr)
22 Taoist energy
23 Be for she
24 Alternative linker
26 Political split
31 Followed leader
36 Stereo component
37 Mistakes
38 Long dash
39 The natural state (abr)
40 Excellent
41 Canadian province
42 Informal you (Fr)
43 Daytime
44 Crystalline mineral
47 Yoda's "Try Not"

49 12th zodiac year
51 Makes a river wall
52 Edge
53 Matrix hero
55 3.14159…
56 Helsinki website suffix
57 Matched _
58 Un-broken hearted response?
61 Your favorite blog

DOWN

1 Canadian rock band
2 Smallest state (abr)
3 Cloepatra's killer
4 Use for emphasis
5 Recent, sort of
6 British greeting
7 Follows Farm or Live
8 Shaker letters
9 US health agency (abr)
10 Singer DiFranco
11 3 suffix
12 Foot part (abr)
13 Scrape by

14 To remove bra
17 Cool cars
23 Unplanned
25 Metal beings collectively?
27 Mushroom type
28 Shorten
29 Hawkeye State (abr)
30 Weather portmanteau
32 Skull and _
33 Shorter dash
34 Nevertheless
35 Knowledgeable
40 Quick _ wink
43 News provider (abr)
45 Apple charge?
46 Red prefix
48 Yoga chant
50 Nice rock
52 Accelerate engine
54 Offs opposite
57 Tofu source
59 Fine
60 _ Dirty Bastard
61 Follows so

February 10, 2008

252. Skull-A-Dance! (and Contest!)

Digital illustration.

After making sure this was actually possible
to do, I offered a prize for the first ten people
who filmed themselves dancing this diagram.
I got submissions from around the world with
people dancing it in a range of styles from
ballet to waltz!

February 11, 2008

253. Skull Bag

Cut and folded tea bag.

February 12, 2008

254. Popskull

Arranged popped popping corn.
15 x 20 in.

February 13, 2008

255. Skull at Play

Paper taped to street sign.

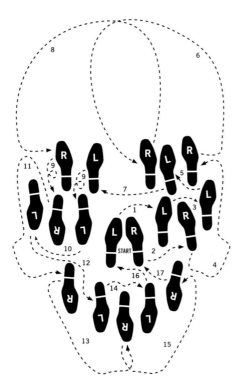

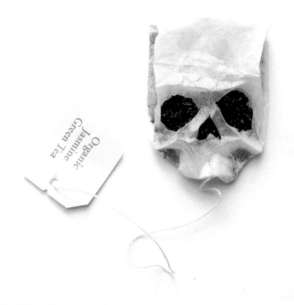

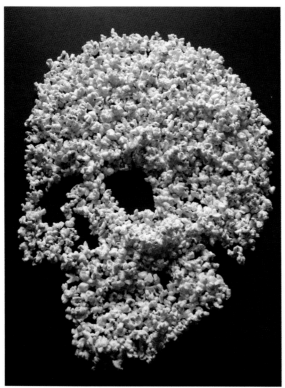

February 14, 2008

256. Brick Skull

Broken and chiseled brick.

February 15, 2008

257. Little Did They Know Skull

Rotated photograph.

I'd walked by this building for years and never noticed the skull hiding in plain sight until I was in the midst of my project.

February 16, 2008

258. Cross-Stitch Skull

Cross-stitched thread on aida fabric.
4 x 4 in.

This one took eight hours of continuous work.

February 17, 2008

259. Sand Painting Skull

Arranged black and white sand. (below) In situ.
7 x 12 in.

I placed a fan on the table next to this piece and documented its gradual disassembly.

February 18, 2008

260. Thread(ed) Skull

Arranged thread.
13 x 18 in.

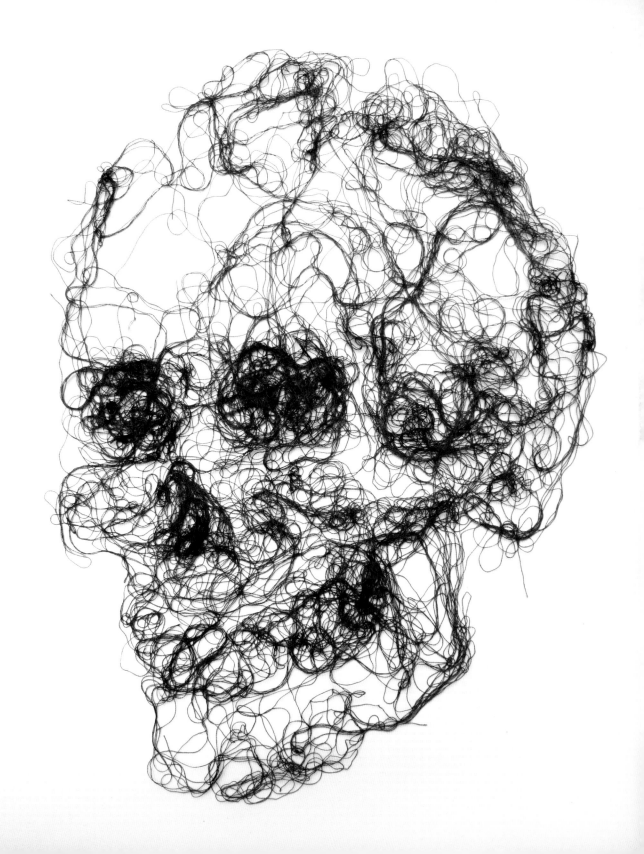

February 19, 2008

261. Skullmouflage

Digital illustration.

February 20, 1998

262. (Alas, Poor Mr.) Potato Skull

Carved potato. (below) Five months later.

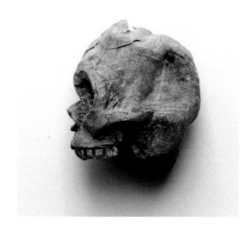

February 21, 2008

263. Drilled Skull

Holes drilled in plywood.
10 x 16 in.

February 22, 2008

264. Bullet Skull

Arranged assorted live 9mm cartridges.
12 x 12 in.

My friend Russ Reed kindly gave me access to his personal collection of ammunition to make this piece.

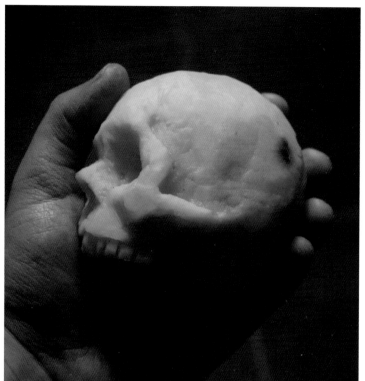
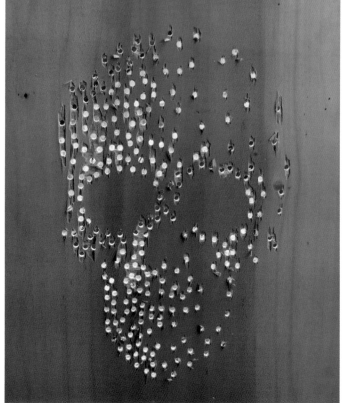
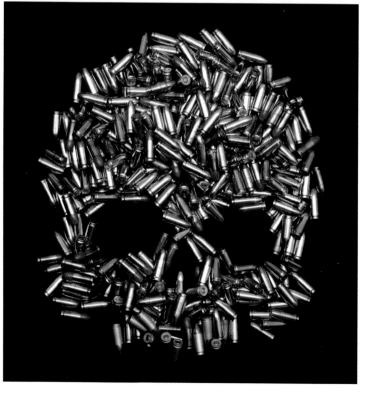

February 23, 2008

265. Bicyskull

Arranged assorted bicycle parts.

Parts courtesy of Kenny Hamilton who also
helped me with the installation in a parking lot
near his house.

February 24, 2008

266. Chess Skull

Arranged chess pieces.

February 25, 2008

267. Skull Chain (Gang)

Arranged bicycle chain.

I only set out to make one skull using the chain, but couldn't help
seeing whether I could make other, more complex views.

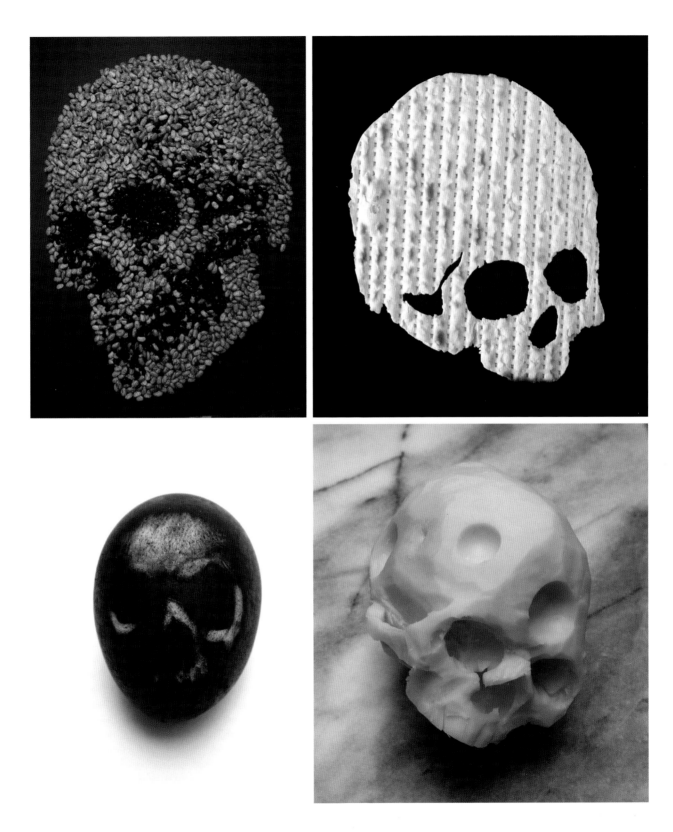

March 2, 2008

273. The Skull or The Vase

Lathe turned aluminum.
3 x 4 x 3 in.

Based on the traditional face or the vase optical illusion. Another piece created with the help of Philip Perrine. Turned from a solid piece of aluminum, this skull took ten hours. The waste from this piece ended up being used for day 275's skull.

March 3, 2008

274. Frog Skull (and Skeleton!)

Cut copper and glass. (below) Kiln fired. 7 x 8 in.

Materials and studio access provided by my friend Carrie Watterworth, who suggested the technique.

March 4, 2008

275. Scrap Metal Skull

Arranged aluminum pieces.
15 x 19 in.

March 5, 2008

276. Skull-Brite

Arranged Lite-Brite pegs. 10 x 5 in.

This Lite-Brite set was actually my sister's childhood toy. I didn't have enough pegs to work with, so I bought some new ones. It turns out the new ones are a different size (and slightly different colors), so I had to hand sand down the new pegs to fit.

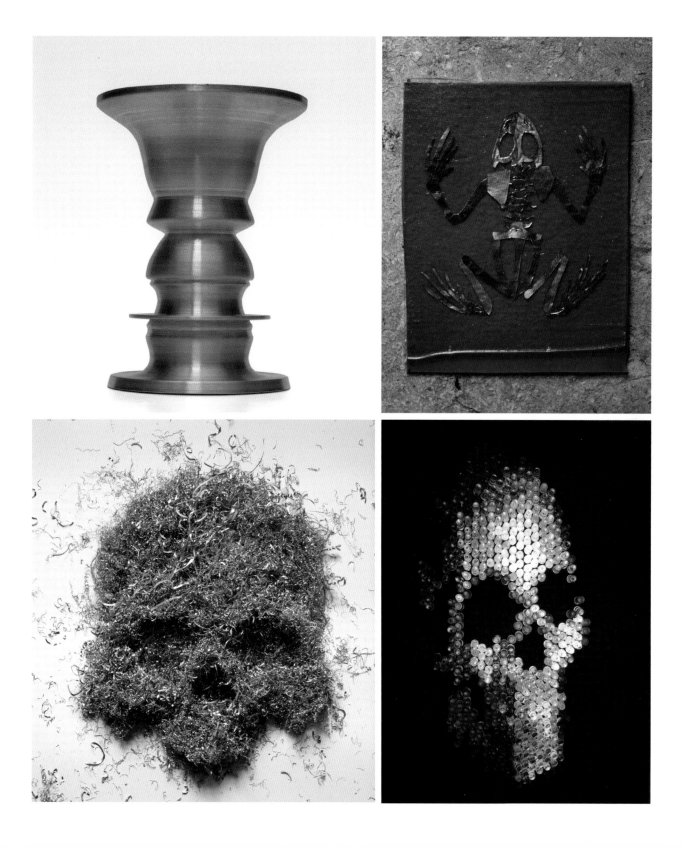

March 6, 2008

277. Circus Skull - for Terry

Arranged "Circus Peanut" candies.
18 x 26 in.

Once again, I was inspired by the work of Bent Object's creator Terry Border after he posted a series of images which featured Circus Peanut candies.

March 7, 2008

278. Untenskull or Skullverware

Arranged forks, knives, and spoons.
20 x 29 in.

March 8, 2008

279. Bouquet of Skull

Arranged cut flowers.
7 x 8.5 ft.

My friend Shelia Gray connected me with a wholesale florist who gave me these flowers that were going to be otherwise discarded. I had to stand on a truck to get far enough away to take this shot from directly above. Afterwards, a couple of neighborhood kids helped dismantle the piece and gave bouquets of the flowers to their grandmother.

March 9, 2008

280. Ticket To Ride Skull

Chalk powder on dirt.
15 x 6 ft.

My friend Bebhinn Neylan suggested I create a piece on a strip of land near her house. This was one of the first times I attempted a large-scale anamorphic installation.

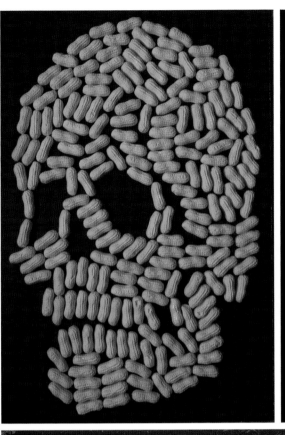

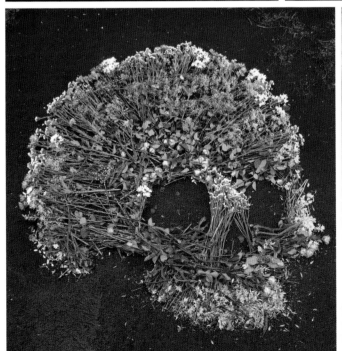

March 11, 2008

282. Pinstripe Skull

Digital illustration. (below) Painted version by Canyon Smith.

March 10, 2008

281. Kneaded Eraskull

Sculpted kneaded eraser.
1.75 x 1.25 x 1.75 in.

Inspired by the art of classic automobile pinstriping, I eventually had this piece painted by an actual practitioner of the art. Canyon customized this car hood for After Life, a 2009 exhibition of the Skull-A-Day project at Quirk Gallery in Richmond, VA.

March 12, 2008

283. Swab the Skull!

2,099 arranged cotton swabs.
26 x 21 in.

March 13, 2008

284. Floating Fabric Skull

Draped glue-infused fabric.
2 ft.

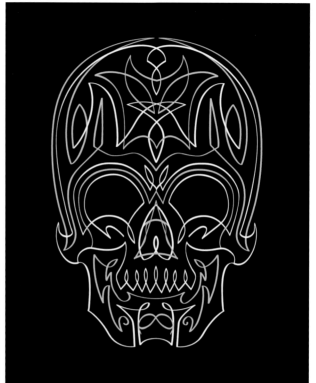
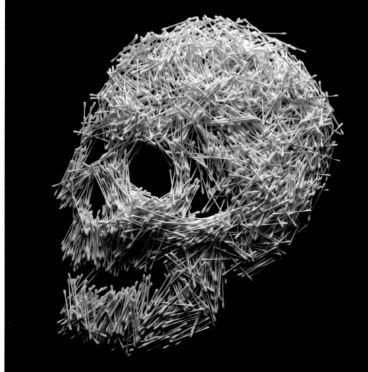

March 14, 2008

285. Oil Paint Skull

Oil paint on wood panel.
6 x 6 in.

This piece reawakened my love for painting
and inspired a yearlong 100 Painted Skulls
Project which I did between 2011 and 2012.

March 15, 2008

286. Piñata Skull

Hand cut tissue paper over papier-mâché.
8 x 12 x 9 in.

Tere taught me her mother's technique for
making piñatas. It was a ten-hour process to
make this piece by hand.

March 16, 2008

287. Chain Link Skull

Fabric woven through chain link fence.
Approx. 4 x 4 ft.

My friend Betsy Migliaccio suggested this location to me and
secured permission to use the fence, which was surrounding the
construction site for a future police precinct.

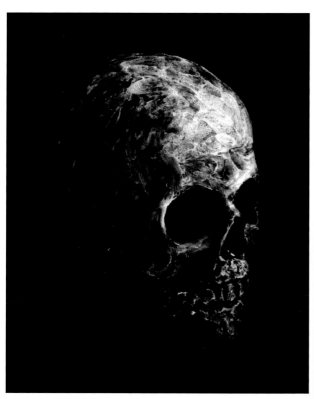

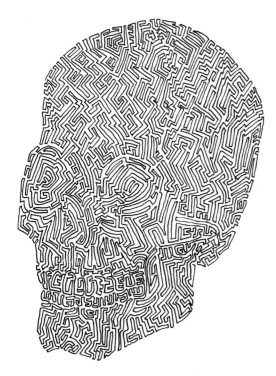

March 21, 2008

292. Found Skull #5: Subway Glob

(left) Photograph of paint and gum subway platform, NYC.
(right) Ballpoint ink on cardboard.

March 22, 2008

293. NYC Fluff Skull

Sculpted found pillow stuffing.

The remnants of a giant public pillow fight
happening across the street in Union Square
in Manhattan.

March 23, 2008

294. Airsickness Skull

Crumpled and torn inverted airsickness bag.
7.5 x 7.5 in.

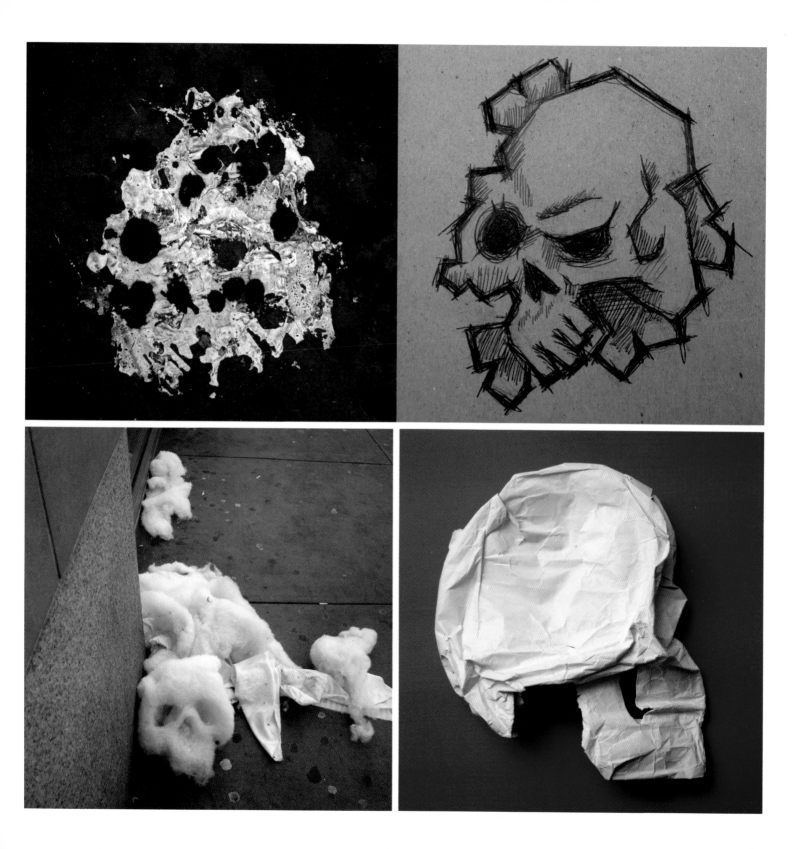

March 24, 2008

295. Shark Tooth Skull (This Time...It's Personal!)

Arranged shark teeth.
10 x 13 in.

John Latell mailed me his personal collection
of shark's teeth to use on this day.

March 25, 2008

296. Connect the Skull (La, La, La, La, La)

Digital illustration. (bottom) Completed.

March 26, 2008

297. (Hot, Hot, Hotter Than) Hot Sauce Skull

Hot sauce on board.
5.5 x 11 in.

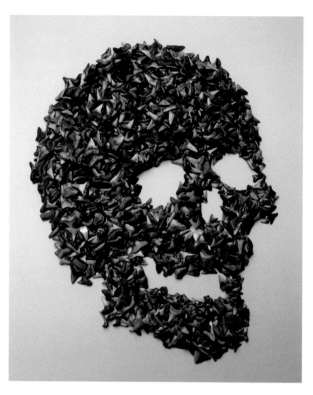

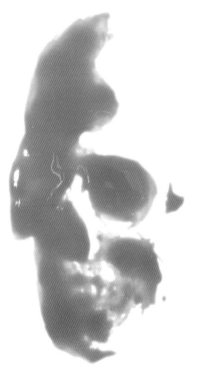

March 27, 2008

298. Lincoln's Skull

Arranged Lincoln Logs.
12 x 7 x 6 in.

March 28, 2008

299. Jumbo Glitter Skull

Arranged glitter.
28 x 10 in.

March 29, 2008

300. Three Hundred Dollar Skull

300 arranged U.S. one dollar bills.
29 x 42 in.

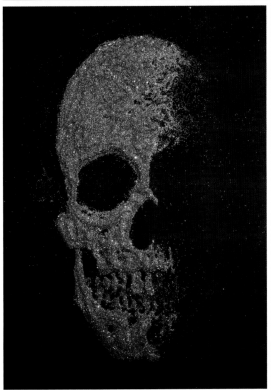

March 31, 2008

302. (Who Watches the) Watch Skull(?)

Arranged watches.
12 x 12 in.

March 30, 2008

301. Tchotchke Skull

Arranged assorted items, Exile, Richmond, VA.
(bottom) Alternate view.
Approx. 3 x 10 ft.

My friend Mimi Regelson invited me to make whatever I wanted in her antique and clothing store (where I had actually worked in my first post-college job). The store, which had been in several locations in Richmond, VA since 1986, eventually closed in 2011.

April 1, 2008

303. A Skull of Letters

Arranged vintage ceramic letters.
14 x 10 in.

Since this was April Fools' Day, before I posted this piece I posted a photograph of a ceramic mug and said I was going to stop making skulls and was going to switch the site from Skull-A-Day to Mug-A-Day. It started a tradition of posting ever-elaborate joke posts on April 1st, the most complicated of which featured a short mockumentary video created by my friend, comedian Eliza Skinner, which featured improv artists rehearsing a fictional musical based on my first book *Skulls*.

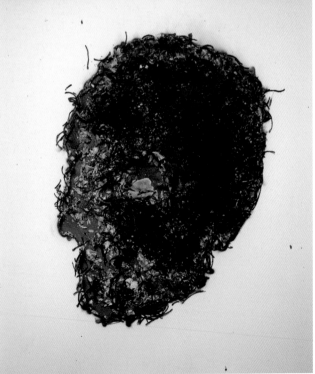

April 2, 2008

304. (Don't Play With) Matches Skull

Arranged matches. (left top) Lit. (left bottom) Burned.
16 x 24 in.

Surprisingly, a pile of matches does not actually burn up that quickly. The entire process of burning this took about fifteen minutes after a few false starts. This is a technique that I have returned to recently to create portraits.

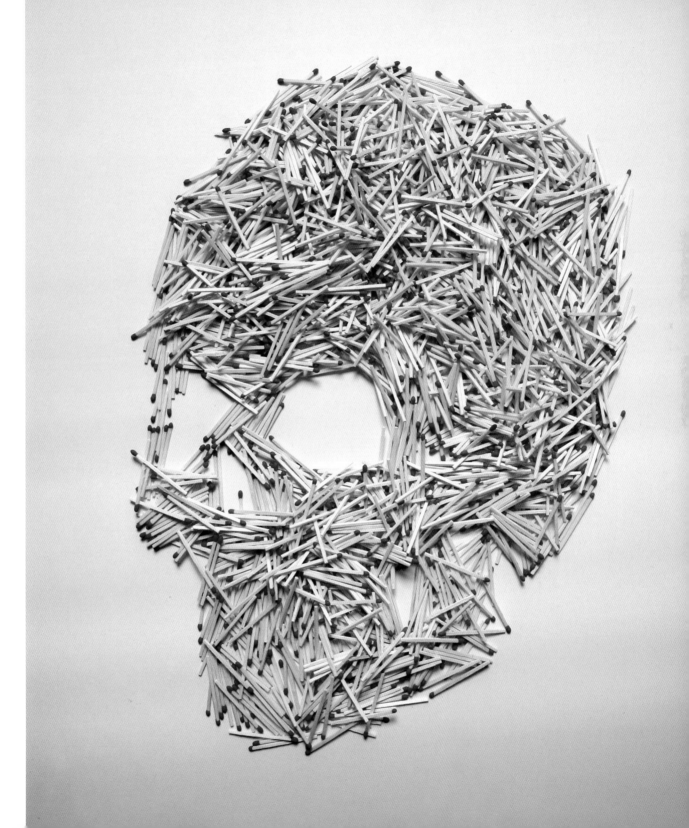

April 3, 2008

305. Neon Skull

Arranged neon signs. (below) In situ.
Approx. 4 x 5 ft.

Neon artist Bob Ziegler kindly let me play
with old signs that were laying around his
workshop. This was a temporary arrangement
on the floor of his studio. The signs had to be
faced downward to prevent the wiring from
shorting out.

April 5, 2008

307. Mr./Ms. Squarehead Skull

Digital illustration.

April 4, 2008

306. Skulltone Pattern

Digital halftone pattern photo-illustration. (below) Detail.

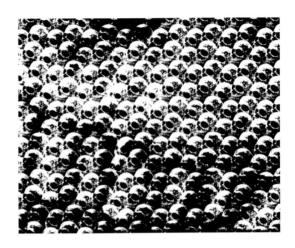

April 6, 2008

308. Lego Skull

Stacked Lego blocks.
6 x 5.5 x 5 in.

This was built from a random set of used
Legos that I bought in an online auction.
I just made up the design as I went along, so
there was no pattern when I was finished.
In 2011 Lego artist Clay Morrow kindly
offered to create a DIY set of instructions for
it, which is available for free, so anyone can
make their own version of this piece.

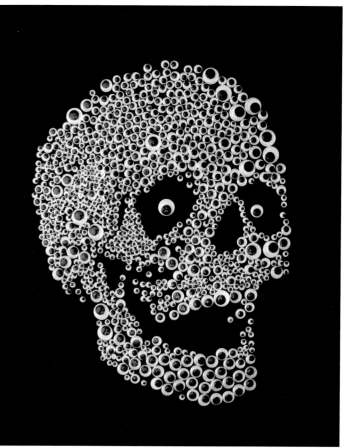

April 10, 2008

312. Quilled Skull

Quilled paper.
5.5 x 6 in.

April 11, 2008

313. Etch-A-Skull

Continuous line Etch-A-Sketch illustration.

I actually managed to preserve this for several years. It only recently got erased on a bumpy car ride back from being on display at a gallery in NYC.

April 12, 2008

314. Skullevision

Acrylic paint on television set. (below) Alternate views.

April 13, 2008

315. Garden Skull

Arranged plants.
Approx. 2 x 2 ft.

My friend Carra gave me access to her yard and helped me with this one, so I left the plants behind for her to keep.

April 22, 2008

324. Audience Skull

Arranged poster board & students.
St. John's University, Queens, NY.

Design teacher and author Aaris Sherin
invited me to come visit her class. As part
of my lecture, I had the students help me
recreate my 8 x 8 design from Day 16. Sadly,
I couldn't get a higher vantage point to
document the end result.

April 23, 2008

325. Tile Skull

Arranged ceramic tiles.
22 x 28 in.

April 24, 2008

326. Pile O' News Skull

Hand carved newspapers.

April 25, 2008

327. Skullringe

Arranged syringes.
16 x 22 in.

My cousin Cheryl collected her insulin
syringes for me to use this day. And yes, I did
manage to get stuck by one in the process.

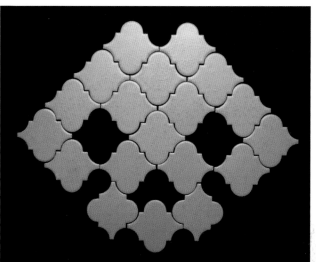

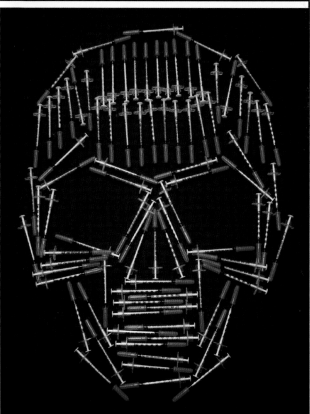

April 26, 2008

328. Rock 'N' Skull

Arranged rocks, Poplar Lawn Park, Petersburg, VA. (above) In situ.
Approx. 8 x 8 ft.

My friend Phil Cheney suggested that I make something in this
park near his house. The rocks were salvaged by him from the creek
running through it. We left it up and it managed to stay there for
several months, during which time the local maintenance crews
would dutifully mow around it.

April 27, 2008

329. Skull-Ray

X-Ray photography.

My friend gave me access to the teaching x-ray equipment at the local medical school where she taught. We did preparatory tests using a "phantom skull" – a real human skull encased in Lucite. We then did three x-rays of my own head with a opossum skull taped to the side of it.

April 28, 2008

330. Bent Objects Skull

Ketchup painting and Bent Objects by Terry Border. (below) Detail.

After getting a great deal of inspiration from Terry's work and discussing the possibility of doing a collaborative piece with him for many months, we finally came up with an idea of how to work together. Terry outlined a concept and mailed me the characters. I then set up the photo and created my addition to the scene.

April 29, 2008

331. Bleach(ed) Skull

Bleach painting on denim.

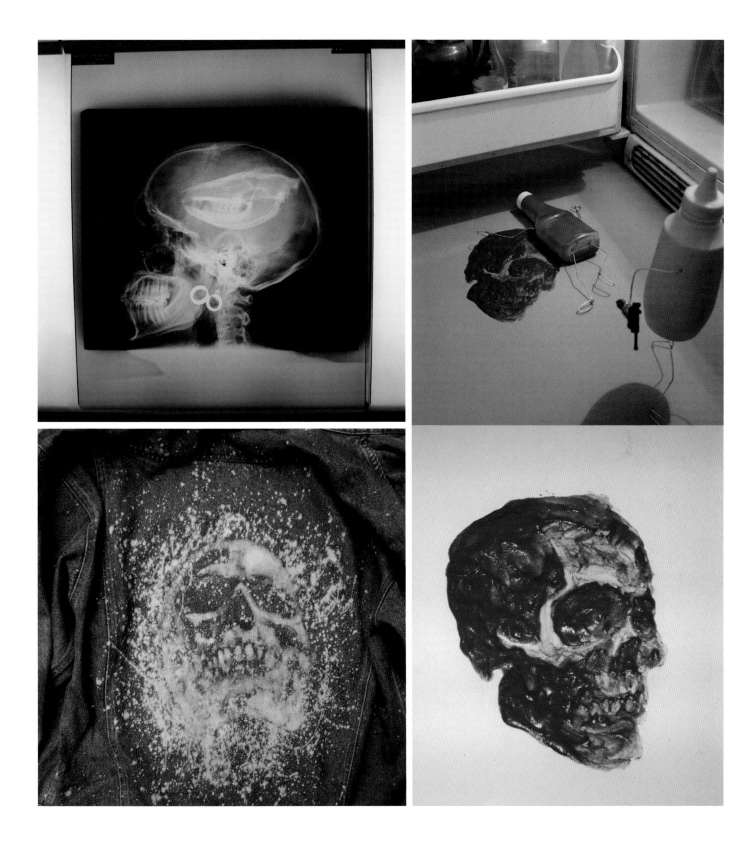

April 30, 2008

332. Topiary Skull

Trimmed boxwood.

Mimi, who had already given me access to her store, also let me do some damage in the name of art to the foliage in front of her own home.

May 1, 2008

333. Oil on Linen Skull

Oil paint on linen canvas.
12 x 12 in.

May 2, 2008

334. (Dies With the Most) Toys Skull

Arranged toys.
25 x 20 in.

My friend Kori Rose dropped off a box of her childhood toys for me to play with this day.

May 3, 2008

335. Tie-"Die" Skull a.k.a. Hippie Skull

Fabric dye on t-shirt.

May 8, 2008

340. Mesh Skull

Hand bent brass mesh.
10 x 16 in.

May 9, 2008

341. Gear (Head) Skull

Arranged Vespa & Lambretta scooter gears,
Scoot Richmond, Richmond, VA.
4.5 x 4.5 ft.

A return to the scooter store thanks to an
invite from Dave (pictured) and his boss
Chelsea Lahmers. I spent a surprising
amount of time at the shop during my project
considering I don't actually own a scooter.

May 10, 2008

342. (Band of the) Hand Skull

Arranged hands, Maymont Park, Richmond, VA.

Once again my friend Madonna (shown)
came through with a great suggestion for
skull making. Featuring the hands of fellow
members of her tribal dance troupe, Caravan
Mystique, and her husband Phil.

May 11, 2008

343. Pop-Up Skull

Cut & folded paper.
5.5 x 10 in.

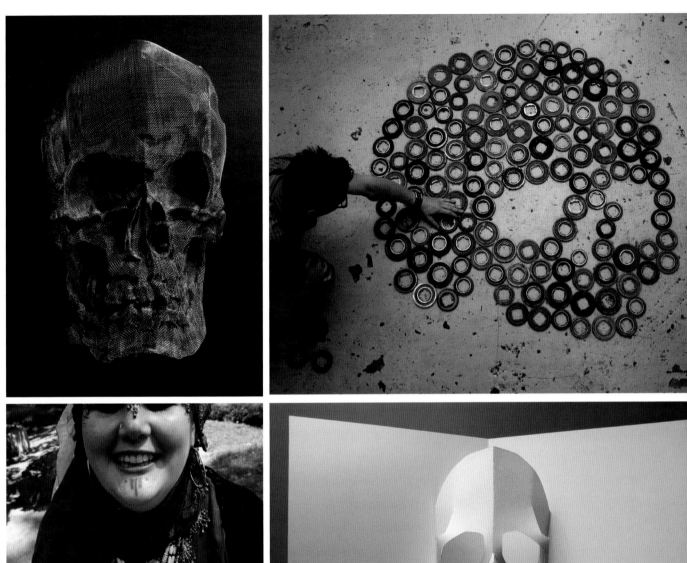

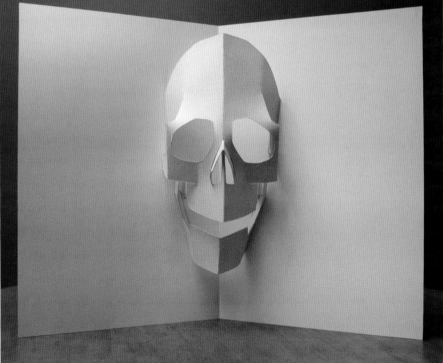

May 12, 2008

344. Bullet Hole Skull

.22 and 9mm bullet holes in aluminum,
Dominion Shooting Range, Richmond, VA.
11 x 13 in.

My friend Russ offered to talk with the owners
of a shooting range to see if I could make
some art there. I shot from about an inch away
for the sake of accuracy.

May 13, 2008

345. Tinkerskull

Arranged Tinkertoys.
11 x 12 x 6 in.

May 14, 2008

346. Bokeh Skull

Bokeh photography using small paper stencil over lens.
(below) Alternate shot.

May 15, 2008

347. Skulledelic a.k.a. May Cause Seizures Skull

Digital illustration.

Another one of the most popular creations of
the year. It was licensed for use on sweaters
and handbags, as well as the cover of a book.
I've also seen it used for tattoos and as a street
art stencil.

May 23, 2008

355. Ultimate Scooter Skull

Arranged scooters and scooter parts.
Scoot Richmond, Richmond, VA.

One more visit to the scooter shop, this time during a "Halloween in May" event. Featuring staff and friends of the shop.

May 24, 2008

356. Skull Trees

Arranged bark on trees.

Anamorphic image created with recently downed trees in the backyard of my relatives Marilyn and Roger's house.

May 25, 2008

357. Nude (but Safe for Work) Skull

Arranged bodies, digital composition.

I knew I wanted to create an homage to Salvador Dalí's famous
image of nude women made into a skull. I didn't want to replicate
his version, but rather create an original take on the concept. In
preparation I reached out to a bunch of figure models and several
agreed to participate. However, none of them showed up the
morning of the shoot. Luckily, at the last minute, two of my friends,
Shelia and Christi, asked about taking part in the shoot as well.
They did double duty by doing two poses, which I then had to stitch
together digitally rather than compose entirely in camera as planned.

May 26, 2008

358. Skull Template

Digital illustration.

May 28, 2008

360. Skull of Cabbage

Carved cabbage. (below) Nine days old.
Approx. 5.5 x 4.5 x 4 in.

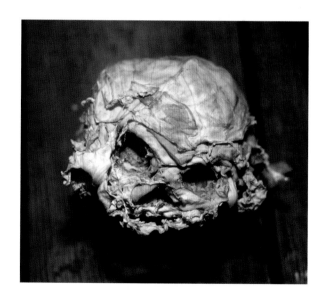

May 27, 2008

359. Pretzskull

Cooked pretzel.
5.5 x 6 in.

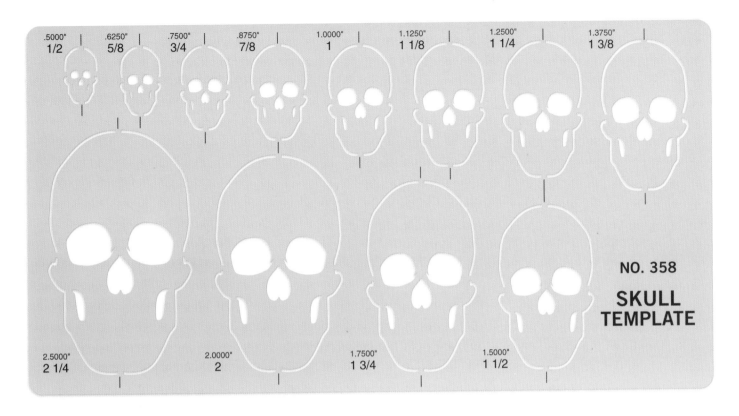

.5000" 1/2 .6250" 5/8 .7500" 3/4 .8750" 7/8 1.0000" 1 1.1250" 1 1/8 1.2500" 1 1/4 1.3750" 1 3/8

NO. 358

SKULL
TEMPLATE

2.5000" 2 1/4 2.0000" 2 1.7500" 1 3/4 1.5000" 1 1/2

May 29, 2008

361. Bakery Skull

Arranged bread, Montana Gold Bread Co., Richmond, VA.

May 30, 2008

362. (Mmmm) Skull Pie

Arranged pie dough, Ipanema Cafe, Richmond, VA. (below) Baked.

May 31, 2008

363. Skullusion

Arranged models and props, Exile, Richmond, VA.

One last visit to Mimi's store. With help from my friends Shelia and Nathan, I created an in-camera version of a classic optical illusion.

Kendra Feather, owner of this favorite local restaurant, invited me into the kitchen to work on one of their famous vegan fruit pies.
I even got to see some patrons eat a slice of the finished creation.

June 1, 2008

364. Group Skull

Arranged people, Belle Isle, Richmond, VA. (above) Alternate version.

I wanted to end the year with a really massive project, so I reached out to my friends and the public through a variety of media and asked for volunteers to create a huge human skull. Ideally, hundreds of people were going to show up, but in reality, early on a Sunday morning is not the best time to ask for volunteers. Ultimately the 32 kind people who did show up were very patient with me and agreed to two poses. First, the best skull I could make with the amount of people I had (above), and then, a representation of the skull I envisioned (right) to which I added a digital shadow to show where the rest of the people would've gone.

June 2, 2008

365. Birthday Skull or (Can You Have Your) Skull Cake (and Eat It Too?)

Frosting on cake.

Because 2008 was a leap year, the 365th day of the project unintentionally ended up being on my birthday. So, of course, I decorated a cake with a skull and then cut it up and ate it with a bunch of my friends.

June 3, 2008

365.25 Leap Skull (right)

Cut paper.

Many of the fans insisted that since it was a leap year I should post another skull to end it on the right day. I felt like I had completed my task the day before, but out of respect to them I created this bookend to the project, copying the technique of the first skull, using the same paper.

366. Citizen Agent Skull (above)

The real day 366 skull was created by my anonymous über-fan Citizen Agent, who had dutifully commented on nearly every post of the year. It marked the start of Skull-A-Day 2.0 in which I shared the original skull creations of the fans every day for an entire year. My assistant was actually the one that discovered this tableaux that had mysteriously been set up in my front lawn overnight. I had encouraged Citizen Agent to take on the task of creating number 366, but never imagined this would be the result. Even though he went on to become an editor of the site for versions 3.0 through 7.0, Citizen Agent still remains anonymous to me and his fellow Skull-A-Day editors.

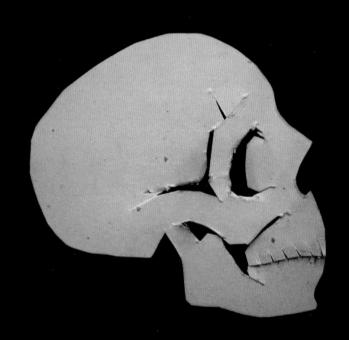

Thank you…

*to all of the wonderful Kickstarter backers who
supported this project;*

*to my intern Megan Maloney for doing the heavy computer lifting
required to get this book ready to print;*

to Ward Tefft for sharing my dream of getting all of my skulls into one book;

and to Jessica & Zinn, whose skulls I love the most.